a taste for all **seasons**

a taste for all **seasons**

carolyn humphries

foulsham
LONDON • NEW YORK • TORONTO • SYDNEY

foulsham

The Publishing House, Bennetts Close, Cippenham, Slough, Berkshire, SL1 5AP, England

Foulsham books can be found in all good bookshops and direct from www.foulsham.com

ISBN: 978-0-572-03299-9

Copyright © 2007 W. Foulsham & Co. Ltd

Illustrations © 2007 Ian P Benfold Haywood

Photographs by Steve Baxter

A CIP record for this book is available from the British Library

Printed in Great Britain by St Edmundsbury Press, Bury St Edmunds, Suffolk

Contents

Let's get back to the real taste of the seasons

Remember the days when we could only buy oranges in winter, apples in the autumn and soft fruits in summer? When brussels sprouts and swedes were winter vegetables and you could only find runner beans from July to September? Now we're so used to being able to buy just about any food at any time of year, imported from all over the world, we forget that every food has a proper season when the flavour, texture, colour and nutritional values are at their peak. For instance, you'll find the best English strawberries in June but parsnips are really not good until the frost has touched them – from November to February – and if you want to taste salmon the way it always used to taste, buy fresh, pale pink wild salmon in the spring rather than the farmed reddish-pink varieties.

Buying British

With modern transportation, we can have food delivered from anywhere in the world any time. The trouble is, in order for us to have it looking just right in our shops, it has often been harvested before it's ready. Compare the taste of a tomato picked green, packed in a box and sent to us from, say, southern Spain, that's just turning from orange to red when it reaches the supermarket, to one that's been ripened on the vine right here. You can smell the difference before you even sink your teeth into its rosy flesh.

Think of a king scallop, sitting amongst a pile of its friends, devoid of shell, probably still half-frozen. Cook it and it'll taste nice. But go to your local fishmonger in the late summer and you may be lucky enough to buy native ones, still sitting in their half shells, their bright orange corals looking as fresh as when they left the sea. Cook them and they'll taste heavenly.

We have a battle to buy British sometimes. We produce fabulous eating apples in the UK but only 20 per cent of apples sold are home grown. Producers are trying to fight back and some are even buying apple-polishing machines in an attempt to make their fruit look more alluring to customers!

Food miles

There are nutritional implications, too. Did you know, for instance, that broccoli from Spain is transported nearly 1,000 miles under refrigerated conditions to get to the UK? This has such an impact on nutrients that experts claim that the broccoli has lost so much goodness that, like peas, the frozen version is healthier! The daft thing is we grow plenty of it in Britain anyway!

Vast quantities of the food we buy have been transported half way round the world to reach us. These 'food miles' have a big impact on climate change because of the pollution the fuel for the transport creates. This is even true of some UK produce, because supermarket chains ferry produce right across the country to a central sorting and packing depot and then transport it again to distribute it to their various stores nationwide (this also creates another environmental issue – huge packaging waste – but that's another story!).

There are, of course, some foods that are not grown commercially or found in the UK – like citrus and tropical fruits and various species of fish – but they, too, have seasons and you'll see in the book when is the best time to buy a whole selection of them. When you can buy home grown, however, not only will the flavour be better than a much-travelled counterpart but you'll be doing your bit for the economy and the environment.

Naturally, there are some basic things that you'll want to eat all year round – like onions or apples, for instance. That's fine but it's still good to know when you can buy British and enjoy them at their best.

Buy local

So if you love food, and care about the planet, it's worth taking the trouble to consider not only what's in season but also what you can buy that's local to you. Look out for farmers' markets (see more information below) – they're springing up all over the place and the foods sold will have been produced in the vicinity and travelled only a short distance, so will be at their peak in every way.

You can also investigate local produce box schemes, where you get a selection of the best fruit and vegetables available for that week at a fixed price. It's a bit of a lottery – you may not like or want three aubergines or six turnips or whatever, but you will get an interesting variety, which is good for creative cookery! When supermarket shopping, read the labels to see where the produce originated – a lot of British-produced foods will have the Union Jack on them for quick reference.

Going organic

If you want to go the whole hog, then choose organic as well. Nutritionally, there is still much debate as to whether organic food has any added value but there's no denying that avoiding chemical fertilisers, pesticides and fungicides is probably a very good thing both for our well-being and the world in general. If you think organic food is just too expensive, remember that the more people demand it, the more will be produced and the cheaper it will become. Go to www.soilassociation.org for more information.

How this book works

This book is divided into the months of the year. Each chapter will tell you what is likely to be in season and what is at its absolute best from the UK.

Of course, the seasons aren't etched in stone (except for closed fishing and game). Weather conditions play a part so you may find local produce slightly earlier or later than I've said (though lots of produce is grown in hothouses or polytunnels to protect it from the elements and extend its season). But the lists will give you a good idea of what time of year to look out for the pick of the crop.

As far as meat is concerned, you can buy excellent British beef, pork, bacon and poultry all year round, so I haven't included these in the lists (though there are some great recipes using them, of course!). I have included British lamb, though. Buy free-range or outdoor-reared meat and poultry whenever you can for the best flavour and quality. The animals' diets make a difference, too. Beef, for instance, is considered at its best from late spring through until autumn, when the cattle are eating fresh grass rather than the silage of the winter. The golden, corn-fed, free-range chickens have, in my opinion, a superior flavour, too. But, be careful, just because a chicken is labelled corn-fed doesn't mean it's free-range so check before you buy.

In the book, for each month you'll find sumptuous recipes using the wonderful variety of foods that are in season: two recipes each for soups, starters and snacks; seafood; meat, game and poultry; vegetables; and desserts. They are all here to start you off on a whole new gourmet journey.

Top tips for buying your food

It's not difficult to make a few changes to your shopping and buying habits in order to make a big change to the quality of your eating. Here are a few simple tips to remember when you're shopping.

- Buy foods that are in season (see each chapter), when appropriate.

- Check the labels on foods for the country of origin and choose UK where possible.

- Select loose produce rather than pre-packed where possible. Not only can you choose the best available but you'll also save on packaging, which helps the environment.

- Visit farmers' markets (see below).

- Buy from farm shops or pick your own. One word of warning ... don't go mad, you can end up buying far more than you want or need and that could be wasteful if you can't freeze or preserve it in some other way.

- Look for local vegetable box/bag schemes. Go to www.ukfoodonline.co.uk or www.alotoforganics.co.uk for details.

- Find local food producers either in yellow pages or on the internet at www.bigbarn.co.uk and www.regionalfoodanddrink.co.uk and www.thefoody.com

- Try to find a local butcher who rears his own meat, rather than buying meat from the supermarket – or buy it from a farmers' market. You can also buy seasonally reared, traceable meats direct from farms online. Just type 'meat farm shop' into your search engine to find one close to home.

Farmers' markets

These are markets where local growers, farmers and producers get together to sell their own produce direct to the customer. There are strict criteria that have to be met: everything must have been grown, reared or produced and processed by the seller.

Shoppers can be sure that they are buying locally produced foods. This usually means within 30 miles (or 50 miles when in large cities or remote towns and villages) from where they were produced. It is recommended that nothing travels more than 100 miles maximum. Game must have been shot locally and must be sold by the licence-holder. Fish should be sold by the fishermen who caught it. Processed foods must contain at least 10 per cent of local produce. Groups, such as the Women's Institute, may have stalls providing that they are the bona fide producers of the goods they are selling and they meet the other criteria.

For further information contact:

National Association of Farmers' Markets, PO BOX 575, Southampton SO15 7BZ

Tel: 0845 45 88 420

Or visit the website at www.farmersmarkets.net

Fairtrade

Consider ethical trading when you shop, too. The Fairtrade Foundation is an independent body offering disadvantaged producers in the developing world a better deal for their produce. Many of the goods – bananas, citrus fruits, mangoes, pineapples, avocados, coffee, tea, cocoa, sugar, spices and rice, to name but some – are not even grown here, so make excellent additions to buying home produce. At least, then, you are also making a much-needed difference by buying them. Look out for this symbol on products:

Notes on the recipes

- The ingredients are listed in the order in which they are used in the recipe.

- All spoon measures are level: 1 tsp=5 ml; 1 tbsp=15 ml.

- Eggs are medium unless otherwise stated.

- Always wash, peel, core and seed, if necessary, fresh produce before use.

- Seasoning and the use of strongly flavoured ingredients such as garlic or chillies are very much a matter of personal taste. Taste the food as you cook and adjust to suit your own palate.

- Use fresh herbs when in season.

- All can and packet sizes are approximate as they vary from brand to brand. For example, if I call for a 400 g large can of tomatoes and yours is only a 397 g can, that's fine.

- Cooking times are approximate and should be used as a guide only. Always check food is piping hot and cooked through before serving.

- Always preheat the oven and cook on the shelf just above the centre unless otherwise stated in the receipe.

Christmas is over and winter has well and truly set in. It's the time of year to enjoy the best of **British root vegetables**, **cabbages**, **leeks** *and* **sprouts**. **Pears** *remain at their best and stored* **apples** *are good, too. Some* **game birds** *are still in season and* **cod** *is in its prime during the winter months. Although not British,* **citrus fruits** *are superb at this time of year, so make the most of them. I recommend making hearty stews or casseroles with lots of root vegetables to keep out the cold but I thought you might also like to try some slightly more unusual recipes, which I've created especially for you in the following pages.*

January

Vegetables

Beetroot, *brussels sprouts, brussels tops, cabbages (green, red and white)*, carrots, celeriac, *celery, chicory*, curly endive, *curly kale, Jerusalem artichokes, leeks*, lettuces, *onions*, pak choi, *parsnips, potatoes (old, maincrop)*, salsify and scorzonera, shallots, spring greens, *swedes*, Swiss chard, turnips

Fruit and nuts

Apples (Cox's, Bramley), avocados (Fuerte), black grapes, clementines, grapefruit, lemons, mangoes, oranges, passion fruit, *pears (Conference, Comice)*, pineapples, pomegranates, satsumas, Seville oranges, tangerines, walnuts

Meat, poultry and game

Duck, goose, guinea fowl, *hare, partridge, pheasant (England, not Scotland), snipe*, venison, wild duck (mallard), *woodcock*, wood pigeon

Fish and seafood

Brill, clams, *cockles, cod*, crabs, haddock, hake, halibut, John Dory, lemon sole, monkfish, mussels, oysters, plaice, turbot, *whiting*

Foods in season

Foods in *italics* are foods from the UK at the peak of their season.

This is a lovely warming soup that tastes really good with some crisp crumbled bacon scattered over it. Alternatively, for a hearty lunch, serve it with a bacon sandwich. You can vary the flavour by substituting two carrots for the parsnip or using half ground coriander and half cumin.

Spiced artichoke and parsnip potage

Serves 4

15 g butter
1 onion, chopped
½ tsp ground cumin
350 g Jerusalem artichokes, cut in
   small chunks
1 large parsnip, cut in small chunks
1 large potato, cut in small chunks
1 litre vegetable or chicken stock,
   ideally fresh or made with
   1 stock cube
1 bouquet garni sachet
Salt and freshly ground black
   pepper
3 tbsp dried milk powder
1 tbsp chopped fresh parsley

1 Melt the butter in a large saucepan. Add the onion and fry over a fairly gentle heat, stirring, for 2 minutes until softened but not browned. Stir in the cumin.

2 Add the remaining vegetables, the stock, bouquet garni and a little salt and pepper. Bring to the boil, reduce the heat, part-cover and simmer for 20 minutes or until the vegetables are really tender. Discard the bouquet garni.

3 Purée in a blender or food processor with the milk powder, then return to the saucepan. Taste and re-season if necessary.

4 Reheat, then ladle into warm bowls. Sprinkle with the parsley and serve hot.

Chicory and orange have always been firm companions. The sweet acidity of the fruit offsets the sometimes bitter vegetable. The salty Halloumi cheese adds another dimension and also makes the dish substantial enough for a light lunch with plenty of crusty bread.

Chicory, leek and orange salad with Halloumi and pine nuts

1 Heat a small frying pan. Add the pine nuts and toss until lightly golden. Tip out of the pan on to a plate to prevent further cooking. Leave to cool.

2 Cut a cone shape out of the base of each head of chicory. Cut the heads in thick chunks and separate into leaves. Put in a bowl with the sliced leek.

3 Cut all the peel and pith off the oranges, holding the fruit over the bowl of vegetables. Cut into slices and then cut each slice in quarters. Add to the vegetables with any juice.

4 Squeeze the membranes over a small separate bowl, to extract the juice.

5 Preheat the grill. Brush the cheese with a little of the oil and place on foil on the grill rack. Grill for about 2 minutes on each side until turning golden.

6 Meanwhile, whisk the remaining oil into the orange juice with the balsamic condiment, mustard and a little salt and pepper. Pour over the salad and toss.

7 Pile in individual bowls, sprinkle the pine nuts over and top with the cheese. Serve straight away.

Serves 4

50 g pine nuts
2 heads of chicory
1 leek, thinly sliced
2 oranges
250 g block Halloumi cheese, cut in 8 slices
4 tbsp olive oil
2 tbsp white balsamic condiment
½ tsp Dijon mustard
Salt and freshly ground black pepper

I was an avid user of pancetta until I discovered that much of it is artificially smoked bacon and often from pigs whose welfare is not of great importance. Consequently, I prefer to use thinly sliced streaky bacon from well-kept British pigs instead. If you do want to use pancetta, make sure it's labelled farm-assured.

Roasted bacon-wrapped cod with melted cheese on cabbage

Serves 4

8 thin rashers of smoked streaky bacon, rinds removed

4 pieces of cod loin, about 175 g each

2 tbsp olive oil

½ tsp dried mixed herbs

Salt and freshly ground black pepper

25 g butter

1 onion, thinly sliced

1 small white cabbage, thinly shredded

1 tbsp caraway or poppy seeds

50 g Cheddar cheese, grated

50 g Gruyère cheese, grated

6 tbsp double cream

8 chive stalks, for garnishing

To serve:

Sautéed potatoes

1 Stretch the bacon with the back of a knife. Wrap each piece of the fish in two rashers, covering as much of the fish as possible. Place, folds down, in a roasting tin and brush all over with the oil. Sprinkle with the herbs and add a good grinding of pepper. Roast in a preheated oven at 220°C/gas 7/fan oven 200°C for 20–25 minutes.

2 Meanwhile, melt the butter in a saucepan. Add the onion and fry, stirring, for 3 minutes until lightly golden.

3 Add the cabbage and toss in the butter until coated. Add a little salt and pepper and the caraway or poppy seeds. Cover and cook very gently for 15 minutes until just tender, stirring occasionally.

4 Put the cheeses and cream in a separate pan. Heat, stirring all the time, until melted and smooth. Do not allow to boil.

5 Remove the fish from the oven. Cut each piece into four thick slices. Spoon the cabbage on to four warm plates. Top each with the pieces of fish and spoon the pan juices over. Trickle the melted cheese around and lay two chive stalks on top of each to garnish. Serve with sautéed potatoes.

If you can't buy fresh cockles, use clams or even mussels. Always pick over the shellfish carefully, discarding any broken or open ones, or those that don't shut when sharply tapped. Discard, too, any that remain closed – or almost closed – after cooking. If using mussels, pull off the top shells before adding to the pasta.

Penne with saffron and fresh cockles

1 Put the cockles in a large saucepan with the wine and water. Bring to the boil, cover and cook for 4–5 minutes, shaking the pan occasionally until the cockles open.

2 Tip into a colander over a bowl. Discard any cockles that haven't opened.

3 Melt the butter with the oil in the rinsed-out saucepan. Add the carrots, onion and garlic and cook gently, stirring, for 2 minutes until softened but not browned.

4 Add the strained mussel liquor and the stock and bring to the boil. Add the pasta, saffron and a little salt and pepper. Stir, bring back to the boil, part-cover and cook for about 10 minutes until the pasta is just tender but still with some 'bite' and the liquid is almost absorbed.

5 Stir in the cockles and half the parsley and heat through gently. Taste and re-season if necessary.

6 Pile on to warm plates and garnish with the remaining chopped parsley.

Serves 4

900 g fresh cockles in their shell, scrubbed
300 ml dry white wine
15 g butter
2 tbsp olive oil
2 carrots, finely diced
1 onion, finely chopped
2 garlic cloves, crushed
300 ml hot chicken, fish or vegetable stock, ideally fresh or made with 1 stock cube
350 g penne pasta
A good pinch of saffron strands
Salt and freshly ground black pepper
A good handful of fresh parsley, chopped

Braised red cabbage is an old favourite but the addition of pear instead of apple and a splash of red wine really lifts it into another category of flavour. Try it with pork, sausages, turkey and venison. You can make a tasty white version, too, substituting white cabbage and wine for the red.

Gammon with grainy mustard sauce on braised red cabbage

Serves 4

½ red cabbage, finely shredded
1 onion, halved and thinly sliced
2 not-too-ripe pears, peeled, cored and chopped
50 g raisins
1 tbsp red wine vinegar
120 ml red wine
2½ tbsp demerara sugar
Salt and freshly ground black pepper
15 g butter
4 gammon steaks
2 tbsp brandy
4 tbsp apple juice
2 tbsp grainy mustard
150 ml crème fraîche
Sprigs of parsley, for garnishing
To serve:
Creamed potatoes

1 Mix the cabbage with the onion, pears and raisins in a saucepan. Add the vinegar, wine, 2 tbsp of the sugar and some salt and pepper. Bring to the boil, stirring, then cover and reduce the heat. Cook gently, stirring occasionally, for about 30 minutes until the cabbage is tender and the liquid has been absorbed.

2 Meanwhile, melt the butter in a large frying pan. Snip the gammon steaks all round the edges with scissors to prevent them curling up. Fry for 2 minutes on each side until cooked through and golden (you may have to do this in two batches). Keep them warm.

3 Stir the brandy into the pan juices with the apple juice. Boil rapidly until reduced by half.

4 Stir in the mustard, crème fraîche and the remaining demerara sugar. Bring to the boil, stirring. Season to taste with salt and pepper.

5 Put the gammon on to warm plates. Spoon the mustard sauce over and top with the red cabbage. Garnish each portion with a sprig of parsley. Serve with creamed potatoes.

The pear and nutmeg relish is lovely with other roast birds, too. To make creamed potatoes with parsnips, simply boil two large potatoes and two large parsnips in boiling lightly salted water. Drain, mash them well and beat in a knob of butter, 3–4 tbsp single cream and a good grinding of black pepper.

Roast partridge with pear and nutmeg relish

1 Put the thyme inside the birds and place them in a roasting tin. Smear the birds with the butter, season lightly and lay the bacon over the breasts. Roast in a preheated oven at 180°C/gas 4/fan oven 160°C for 45 minutes.

2 Meanwhile, make the relish. Heat the oil in a small pan. Add the onion and fry, stirring, over a moderate heat for 4 minutes until soft and lightly golden. Add the pear, sugar and condiment, bring to the boil, stir and cook rapidly for 4–5 minutes until the pear is soft but still holds its shape and most of the liquid has evaporated. Add freshly grated nutmeg to taste, then stir in the parsley. Tip into a small dish and reserve.

3 When the partridge are cooked, remove from the roasting tin and keep warm. Add the cider and the stock to the roasting tin juices. Bring to the boil and boil rapidly, scraping up any sediment in the bottom of the pan, until reduced by half. Season to taste.

4 Transfer the partridge to warm serving plates and spoon the cider gravy over. Put a spoonful of the pear relish on each plate and garnish the plates with sprigs of parsley.

5 Serve with creamed potatoes and parsnips and curly kale.

Serves 4

½ tsp dried thyme
4 oven-ready partridge
25 g butter
Salt and freshly ground black pepper
8 rashers streaky bacon
150 ml medium cider
150 ml chicken stock, fresh or made with ½ chicken stock cube
For the relish:
1 tbsp sunflower oil
1 onion, chopped
2 pears, peeled, cored and chopped
4 tbsp demerara sugar
4 tbsp white balsamic condiment
Freshly grated nutmeg
2 tbsp chopped fresh parsley
Sprigs of parsley, for garnishing
To serve:
Creamed potatoes with parsnips and shredded curly kale

Ideally use a food processor with a thick grating attachment to finely shred all the vegetables but, alternatively, you can use a coarse hand grater though the texture won't be quite as good. This is a lovely accompaniment to cold meats or cheese and tastes great with the addition of a chopped Cox's apple and a handful of chopped walnuts.

Cabbage and celeriac slaw with sweet mustard mayonnaise

Serves 4

2 tbsp mayonnaise
2 tbsp sunflower oil
1 tbsp white wine vinegar
1 tsp demerara sugar
$\frac{1}{2}$ tsp made English mustard
A good pinch of salt and freshly
  ground black pepper
$\frac{1}{4}$ smallish white cabbage, finely
  shredded
$\frac{1}{4}$ celeriac, finely shredded
1 carrot, finely shredded
1 small onion, grated

1 Whisk the mayonnaise with the oil, vinegar, sugar, mustard, salt and pepper in a large bowl.

2 Add all the prepared vegetables and mix thoroughly.

3 Chill until ready to serve.

Photograph opposite:
Gammon with grainy mustard
sauce on braised red cabbage
(see page 22)

I like to use small parsnips when I can for this dish because the large ones tend to have 'woodier' centres, which don't give such a soft, luxurious result. This dish is lovely with roast beef but equally good with roast ham, chicken or pork. You can add a small handful of finely chopped walnuts for a nutty texture, if you like.

Creamy parsnip bake with freshly grated nutmeg

1 Melt the butter in a frying pan. Add the onion and fry gently for 2 minutes, stirring, until softened but not browned.

2 Layer the parsnips with the fried onion in a lightly buttered 1 litre ovenproof dish. Season lightly between each layer with salt, pepper and just a tiny grating of nutmeg.

3 Pour the cream over the top. Cover with foil and bake in a preheated oven at 180°C/gas 4/fan oven 160°C for 1 hour.

4 Remove the foil and bake for a further 15–20 minutes until lightly golden and the parsnips are soft. Serve hot.

Serves 4

15 g butter, plus extra for greasing
1 onion, sliced
4 small parsnips, thinly sliced
Salt and freshly ground black pepper
A little freshly grated nutmeg
300 ml double cream

Photograph opposite:
Braised steak with parsnips and crushed creamed brussels sprouts (see page 35)

This is such an easy dessert to make and yet it's elegant enough for any dinner party. The trick with the fondant is to make it before the tarts to allow it to get cold (but don't chill it). As it cools it thickens until it's gloriously smooth and rich. It's a lovely chocolate sauce to serve warm, too, with ice-cream.

Pear and lemon puff tarts with bitter chocolate fondant

Serves 4

For the fondant:
100 g plain chocolate with 70 per cent cocoa solids
2 tbsp golden syrup
175 ml double cream
For the tarts:
1 sheet of frozen ready-rolled puff pastry, just thawed
4 tbsp lemon curd
2 ripe pears
1 tbsp milk
2 tbsp icing sugar

1 Make the fondant. Melt the chocolate with the syrup in a bowl over a pan of hot water. Heat the cream in a saucepan until it feels just warm to the touch. Whisk into the melted chocolate. Leave to cool until the tarts are ready to serve. The mixture should be thick and smooth.

2 Cut four rounds out of the pastry, using a lid or small saucer as a guide. Transfer to a dampened baking sheet.

3 Spread the lemon curd in the centre of the pastry rounds, leaving a narrow border all round.

4 Peel, halve and core the pears. Put a half on each tart. Brush all over with the milk. Dredge with the sifted icing sugar. Bake in a preheated oven at 220°C/gas 7/fan oven 200°C for about 20 minutes until the pastry is risen and golden round the edges.

5 Remove from the oven and leave to cool for 5–10 minutes. Transfer the warm tarts to serving plates and spoon the fondant around.

This is a wonderful, light, refreshing dessert, ideal for rounding off a heavy meal. The grenadine syrup gives it a bright reddish-orange colour and enhances the flavour no end. The passion fruit adds fragrance and the lemon just cuts through the sweetness, making the balance perfect.

Oranges in grenadine and passion fruit jelly

1 Put the gelatine in a bowl with 2 tbsp of water. Leave to soften for 5 minutes. Stand the bowl in a pan of hot water and stir until dissolved, or heat briefly in the microwave.

2 Halve the passion fruit. Scoop the pulp into a sieve over a measuring jug and rub through, leaving the seeds in the sieve.

3 Thinly pare the zest off one of the oranges and cut into thin strips. Boil the zest in water for 2 minutes, drain, rinse with cold water and drain again. Squeeze the juice from that orange and the lemon in with the passion fruit juice.

4 Hold the remaining oranges over the jug and cut off all the peel and pith, catching any juice in the jug, then separate the fruit into segments. Place the segments in four wine goblets. Squeeze the membranes over the jug to extract the remaining juice. Add the grenadine syrup.

5 Stir in the dissolved gelatine and make up to 450 ml with water. Pour over the fruit in the glasses, then chill until set.

6 Top each with a spoonful of crème fraîche and decorate with the orange shreds.

Serves 4

15 g powdered gelatine
Water
2 passion fruit
4 oranges
1 lemon
6 tbsp grenadine syrup
4 tbsp crème fraîche

We're still in winter and the **roots** and **greens** are the best buys. Tall, thin, pink forced **rhubarb** stalks are appearing and you may see the first early **cauliflowers** (though they usually come into their own next month). **Comice pears** are still very good and you can enjoy **citrus** and other **tropical fruits** including **passion fruit** and **pomegranates** from afar. **Seville oranges** are in, so get making that marmalade! The game bird season is over and **hare** is the only seasonal meat that's at its peak. So it's a time to enjoy **British pork** and **beef** and **free-range chicken**.

February

Vegetables

Brussels sprouts, brussels tops, cabbages (green, white, red), carrots, cauliflowers, celeriac, celery, chicory, *curly endive, curly kale, Jerusalem artichokes, leeks,* lettuces, *onions,* parsnips, potatoes (old or maincrop), *rhubarb (forced),* salsify and scorzonera, shallots, *spring and winter greens, swedes,* Swiss chard

Fruit and nuts

Apples (Cox's, Bramleys), avocados (Fuerte), bananas, blood oranges, kiwi fruit, lemons, mangoes, oranges, passion fruit, *pears (Comice),* pineapples, pomegranates, Seville oranges

Meat, poultry and game

Guinea fowl, *hare,* suckling pig, venison

Fish and seafood

Brill, brown shrimps, clams, *cockles, cod, cod's roe,* crabs, haddock, hake, halibut, John Dory, lemon sole, *mussels,* oysters, salmon, turbot

Foods in season

Foods in *italics* are foods from the UK at the peak of their season.

This is an Italian speciality to which I've given a British twist. Adding parsnip and swede really enhances the flavour and this soup is a great way of contributing to your five-a-day! To make it more Italian, sprinkle it with freshly grated Parmesan instead of the Cheddar.

Mixed vegetable soup with macaroni

Serves 4

2 tbsp olive oil
1 onion, finely chopped
1 leek, thinly sliced
1 celery stick, finely chopped
1 carrot, finely diced
½ small swede, finely diced
1 small parsnip, finely diced
400 g can of chopped tomatoes
1 vegetable stock cube
1 tbsp tomato purée
½ tsp dried oregano
A good pinch of caster sugar
Salt and freshly ground black pepper
50 g short-cut macaroni
Finely grated Cheddar cheese, for garnishing

1 Heat the oil in a large saucepan. Add the onion and leek and fry, stirring, for 2 minutes.

2 Add the remaining vegetables and stir over a gentle heat for 1 minute.

3 Add the can of tomatoes, 2 canfuls of water, the stock cube, tomato purée, oregano, sugar and some salt and pepper. Bring to the boil, stirring, reduce the heat, part-cover and simmer for 20 minutes.

4 Add the macaroni and cook for a further 10 minutes until everything is really tender.

5 Taste and re-season if necessary. Ladle into warm bowls and serve sprinkled with grated Cheddar cheese.

Polenta is simply cornmeal. I use the pre-cooked variety that takes only minutes to turn into the traditional northern Italian side dish. It makes a lovely crisp coating for cheese and for pieces of meat or fish, too. In fact, I prefer it as a coating to the more usual way of serving it!

Polenta-crusted Camembert with fresh lemon and apple chutney

1 Cut the lemon in half, discarding any pips. Finely chop the fruit including the pith and peel. Place in a saucepan with the water and cinnamon stick. Bring to the boil, reduce the heat, cover and simmer very gently for 15 minutes until really tender.

2 Peel, quarter, core and finely chop the apple. Add to the lemon with the sugar and vinegar. Stir until the sugar dissolves. Bring to the boil, reduce the heat, cover and simmer gently for 2–3 minutes until the apple is tender but still has a little shape and the mixture is thick, stirring once or twice. Leave to cool.

3 Cut the Camembert into eight wedges. Coat each one in the flour. Put the beaten egg on a plate. On a separate plate, mix the polenta with the thyme, a little salt and plenty of pepper.

4 Dip each cheese wedge in beaten egg, then the polenta mixture to coat completely. If necessary, dip and coat a second time. Chill until ready to cook.

5 When ready to serve, spoon the lemon chutney into four small pots. Put a small handful of salad leaves and some celery sticks on each of four small wooden platters or plates. Heat about 2.5 cm oil in a large frying pan. Add the cheese wedges and fry for 1–2 minutes on each side until golden brown. Drain on kitchen paper. Transfer to the platters, put a pot of chutney to one side and serve straight away with French bread.

Serves 4

For the chutney:
1 lemon, washed
5 tbsp water
1 small piece of cinnamon stick
1 Cox's apple
50 g granulated sugar
4 tsp white wine vinegar
For the cheese:
250 g firm Camembert round
2 tbsp plain flour
1 large egg, beaten
75 g instant polenta
1 tsp dried thyme
Salt and freshly ground black pepper
Mixed salad leaves and a few celery sticks, cut in short lengths, for garnishing
Groundnut or corn oil for frying
To serve:
French bread or crisp flat breads

Mussels are one of my favourite foods and this is the season for them at their very best. You can, of course, just cook them in the usual way, à la marinière, with a little chopped onion, a splash of white wine and chopped parsley but try this wonderful creation instead – it's so good!

Mussels with white wine, chillies and chorizo

Serves 4

1.75 kg mussels, scrubbed and
   bearded
40 g butter
1 onion, finely chopped
1 leek, finely chopped
1 garlic clove, crushed
150 ml dry white wine
1 red chilli, seeded and chopped
100 g piece of chorizo sausage,
   skinned and finely diced
Freshly ground black pepper
2 tbsp chopped fresh parsley
To serve:
Crusty bread

1 Discard any mussels that are damaged, open or don't close when sharply tapped with a knife.

2 Heat the butter in a large saucepan. Add the onion, leek and garlic and fry over a gentle heat, stirring, for 2 minutes until softened but not browned.

3 Add the wine, chilli, chorizo and a good grinding of pepper. Tip in the mussels.

4 Cover, bring to the boil, reduce the heat to moderate and cook for 4–5 minutes, shaking the pan occasionally, until the mussels have opened. Discard any that remain closed.

5 Ladle into wide soup bowls. Scatter the parsley over and serve with lots of crusty bread.

Matelotes were traditionally made from freshwater fish but I've chosen to use sea fish instead. They always contain whole baby onions and mushrooms and a garnish of fried bread and can, sometimes, have the addition of a few freshwater crayfish to finish the dish. Use any mixture of fish fillets you like.

Matelote of sea fish in Pernod

1 Melt 15 g of the butter in a large deep frying pan and brown the shallots all over. Lift out of the pan with a draining spoon.

2 Crush one of the garlic cloves and add to the pan with the chopped leek, carrots and lardons. Fry gently, stirring, for 2 minutes.

3 Add the cider, stock, Pernod and bouquet garni sachet. Top with the shallots and the mushrooms. Season lightly. Bring to the boil, reduce the heat, cover and cook gently for 8 minutes. Lay the fish on top in a single layer. Re-cover and cook for a further 8 minutes until the fish and vegetables are tender.

4 Meanwhile, cut the other garlic clove in half and rub all over the slice of white bread. Cut the bread into eight triangles. Heat a little oil in a separate frying pan and fry the bread until golden on both sides. Drain on kitchen paper.

5 Mash the remaining butter with the flour to a smooth paste. Carefully lift out the fish with a fish slice and arrange in large shallow soup bowls. Remove the onions and mushrooms and reserve. Keep warm. Discard the bouquet garni.

6 Whisk the butter mixture into the sauce. Boil, whisking, for 2 minutes. Pour over the fish. Garnish with onions, mushrooms and fried bread.

Serves 4

40 g unsalted butter
12 shallots, peeled
2 garlic cloves
1 leek, finely chopped
2 carrots, finely chopped
50 g lardons (diced bacon)
300 ml dry cider
150 ml fish or chicken stock, ideally fresh or made with ½ stock cube
2 tbsp Pernod
1 bouquet garni sachet
100 g whole button mushrooms
Salt and freshly ground black pepper
225 g piece each of cod, salmon and smoked haddock fillet, skinned and cut into 4 pieces
1 slice of white bread
A little sunflower oil
3 tbsp plain flour
4 tbsp single cream

This dish is very good with rabbit – or even beef – too so you don't have to keep it as a once-in-a-rare-while dish. Rabbit will take about 1½ hours to cook. You can vary the recipe by using brown beer or even red wine instead of the Guinness. Cooking greens in this way keeps their lovely colour and nearly all the nutrients.

Hare with Guinness, prunes and mustard on wilted greens

Serves 4–6

4 tbsp plain flour
Salt and freshly ground black
  pepper
1 oven-ready hare, cut into 6 joints
2 tbsp sunflower oil
15 g butter
1 onion, chopped
1 celery stick, chopped
2 tsp Dijon mustard
330 ml can of Guinness
1 beef stock cube
100 g button mushrooms, sliced
100 g ready-to-eat prunes, halved
  and stoned
1 bay leaf
For the greens:
450 g spring greens, coarsely
  shredded, discarding any thick
  stalks
To serve:
Mashed potatoes

1 Mix the flour with a little salt and pepper and use to coat the hare joints.

2 Heat half the oil in a flameproof casserole and brown the hare on all sides. Remove from the casserole.

3 Add the remaining oil and the butter to the casserole and fry the onion and celery, stirring, for 3 minutes until lightly golden.

4 Stir in any remaining flour, the mustard, Guinness and stock cube and bring to the boil.

5 Return the hare to the dish with the mushrooms and prunes. Tuck in the bay leaf. Transfer to a preheated oven at 160°C/gas 3/fan oven 145°C and cook for 2–2½ hours until really tender and bathed in a rich, thick sauce. Discard the bay leaf, taste and re-season, if necessary.

6 When the hare is nearly ready, put the greens in a saucepan with just a pinch of salt. Pour on just enough boiling water from the kettle to soak them and bring back to the boil. Stir well and boil for 1 minute until wilted but still with some 'bite'. Drain thoroughly in a colander.

7 Pile the wilted greens on four plates. Top with the hare and sauce. Serve with fluffy mashed potatoes.

Beef and parsnips are always a perfect combination. Here they are slow-cooked together to melting tenderness. This way of cooking brussels sprouts renders them sweet and delicate – a far cry from the bitter bullets or soggy lumps we were served as children!

Braised steak with parsnips and crushed creamed brussels sprouts

1 Heat the oil in a flameproof casserole. Add the steak and brown quickly on both sides. Remove from the dish.

2 Add the onions and parsnip and fry, stirring, for 3 minutes until lightly golden.

3 Stir in the flour and cook for 1 minute. Remove from the heat and blend in the stock. Return to the heat and bring to the boil, stirring.

4 Return the steak to the pan, tucking it well down in the sauce. Add the bouquet garni and a little salt and pepper.

5 Transfer to a preheated oven at 160°C/gas 3/fan oven 145°C and cook for 1½ hours until the steak and parsnips are really tender. Discard the bouquet garni, taste and re-season, if necessary. Thin the sauce with a little water if too thick.

6 Meanwhile, cook the sprouts in about 2.5 cm of boiling water for 6-8 minutes until just tender but still bright green. Drain and tip into a blender or food processor. Add the butter, cream and a little salt and pepper and run the machine, stopping and scraping down the sides until a rough purée is formed.

7 Reheat in the saucepan. Pile the crushed sprouts on warm plates. Lay a piece of steak to one side and spoon the gravy over. Serve with jacket-baked potatoes and horseradish relish.

Serves 4

1 tbsp sunflower oil
4 frying steaks
2 onions, chopped
1 large parsnip, diced
3 tbsp plain flour
450 ml beef stock, ideally fresh or made with 1 stock cube
1 bouquet garni sachet
Salt and freshly ground black pepper
For the purée:
450 g brussels sprouts
15 g butter
2 tbsp double cream
To serve:
Jacket-baked potatoes and horseradish relish

These are lovely as a substantial starter (without the accompaniment) or light lunch or supper. As a main meal, you may like to serve a jacket potato, too. You can ring the changes by sprinkling the tartlets with blue cheese instead of Cheddar or add extra flavour with a garlic and herb or black pepper soft cheese.

Cheese and leek tartlets with fresh sage

Serves 4

1 sheet of frozen, ready-rolled puff
  pastry, just thawed
25 g butter
2 smallish leeks, thickly sliced
1 egg
100 g white soft cheese
Salt and freshly ground black
  pepper
2 tsp chopped fresh sage
25 g Cheddar cheese, grated
4 small sprigs of sage, for
  garnishing
To serve:
Cabbage and Celeriac Slaw with
  Sweet Mustard Mayonnaise (see
  page 24)

1 Cut the pastry into quarters. Score a line all round each rectangle about 2 cm/³/₄ in from the outer edge to form a rim on each tart, but don't cut right through the pastry. Place on a dampened baking sheet. Chill while preparing the leeks.

2 Melt the butter in a saucepan. Add the leeks and fry, stirring, for 2 minutes until slightly softened. Turn down the heat, cover and cook gently for 4 minutes until almost tender but still with some texture. Tip on to a plate and leave to cool.

3 Preheat the oven to 220°C/gas 7/fan oven 200°C. Beat the egg and use a little to brush round the rim of each pastry rectangle. Bake the pastry cases for 10 minutes until puffy and golden. Gently press down the centres.

4 Beat the soft cheese into the remaining egg with some salt and pepper and the sage. Spread the mixture into the centre of the pastry rectangles, leaving the rims clear. Arrange the leeks over the top and then sprinkle with the Cheddar.

5 Turn down the heat to 190°C/gas 5/fan oven 170°C and bake for a further 15 minutes until the filling is set and the pastry is a rich golden brown.

6 Transfer the tartlets to warm plates and serve with Cabbage and Celeriac Slaw.

You can use scorzonera instead but it's best to cook it unpeeled and peel off the black skin after cooking. Serve this as a vegetarian main course or as an accompaniment to grilled chicken or fish. This is also lovely made with celeriac (in which case, cook for 10 minutes) or courgettes (cook for 4 minutes) instead of the salsify.

Salsify and macaroni casserole with mushrooms

1 Scrub or scrape the salsify and cut into bite-sized chunks. Boil in lightly salted water for 25–30 minutes until just tender. Drain.

2 Meanwhile, cook the macaroni in boiling, lightly salted water in a separate pan for 8–10 minutes until only just tender. Drain well in a colander.

3 Melt the butter in the rinsed-out macaroni pan and fry the onion for 2 minutes, stirring. Add the mushrooms and cook for a further minute. Stir in the flour and cook for 1 minute, stirring.

4 Remove from the heat and blend in the wine, stock, tomatoes and sugar. Bring to the boil, stirring. Add the basil and some salt and pepper to taste. Reduce the heat and simmer gently for 5 minutes.

5 Add the cooked salsify and macaroni, stir gently, cover and simmer over a fairly gentle heat for 5 minutes.

6 Serve sprinkled with grated Cheddar, in pasta bowls.

Serves 4–6

450 g salsify
Salt and freshly ground black pepper
225 g short-cut macaroni
25 g butter
1 onion, chopped
100 g button mushrooms, sliced
2 tbsp plain flour
150 ml dry white wine
150 ml vegetable stock, ideally fresh or made with $\frac{1}{2}$ stock cube
400 g can of chopped tomatoes
A good pinch of caster sugar
$\frac{1}{2}$ tsp dried basil
50 g Cheddar cheese, grated

I love Banoffee Pie but, after the first slice has been cut, somehow the rest always looks a mess as you serve it. Here I've used the same ingredients but layered them in sundae glasses for an elegant dessert that will look just as good as it tastes. You could experiment with pears instead of bananas for a change.

Banana and toffee cream layer dessert

Serves 4

350 g can of sweetened condensed milk
75 g digestive biscuits, finely crushed
25 g butter, melted
4 bananas
2 tsp lemon juice
200 ml crème fraîche
2 tsp drinking chocolate powder

1 Boil the unopened can of condensed milk in a pan of water for at least 2 hours. Lift out of the pan, leave to cool, then chill.

2 Mix the crushed biscuits with the butter.

3 Slice the bananas fairly thinly and toss in the lemon juice.

4 Put half of the banana slices in four tall sundae glasses. Top with half the biscuits then half the toffee-like condensed milk then half the crème fraîche. Repeat the layers.

5 Dust the tops with the chocolate powder, then chill until ready to serve.

Blood oranges are usually extremely juicy, so make the ideal fruit to squeeze for this light fluffy mousse. Topping it with pomegranate pips looks exciting and adds another taste and texture but you could omit them if you prefer or try other contrasting fruits such as sliced bananas, tossed in lemon juice.

Blood orange and fresh pomegranate mousse

1 Put the gelatine in a bowl. Stir in the water and leave to soften for 5 minutes, then stand the bowl in a pan of hot water and stir until completely dissolved or heat briefly in the microwave but do not allow to boil.

2 Halve the oranges and squeeze the juice into a measuring jug; if necessary, make up to 300 ml with pure orange juice. Stir in the dissolved gelatine.

3 Whisk the egg whites until stiff and whisk in 1 tbsp of the icing sugar. Whip the cream until softly peaking.

4 Put the remaining icing sugar in with the egg yolks and whisk over a pan of hot water until thick and pale and the whisk leaves a trail when lifted out of the mixture.

5 Stir in the orange juice. Chill until it's the consistency of unbeaten egg white then fold in half the whipped cream and then the egg whites.

6 Turn into a glass serving dish, then chill until set.

7 Halve the pomegranates and scoop the seeds into a bowl, discarding the membranes as you go.

8 Spread the remaining whipped cream on top of the mousse and top with a pile of pomegranate seeds.

Serves 4–6

1 sachet powdered gelatine
2 tbsp water
4 blood oranges
Pure orange juice
2 eggs, separated
50 g icing sugar, sifted
300 ml double cream
2 pomegranates

This is the beginning of spring. **Cauliflowers** and **leeks** are plentiful and new crops of **purple sprouting broccoli** and **spring greens** are fantastic this month. You'll still get some **roots** – **carrots** and **swedes** in particular – and forced **rhubarb** is in abundance. The last of the **British apples** are available but it's mostly the time for **tropical fruits** to be enjoyed. There's nothing much seasonal in the way of meat this month and **cockles** and **sea trout** are amongst the best local buys from your fishmonger.

March

Vegetables

Cabbages (green), carrots, cauliflowers, *chicory, leeks*, lettuces, onions, potatoes (old, maincrop), *purple sprouting broccoli, radishes, rhubarb (forced)*, shallots, *spring greens*, spring onions, *swedes*, Swiss chard

Fruit and nuts

Apples (Cox's, Bramleys), avocados (Fuerte), bananas, blood oranges, kiwi fruit, lemons, mangoes, oranges, passion fruit, pineapples, pomegranates

Meat, poultry and game

Hare

Fish and seafood

Brown shrimps, *cockles*, cod, hake, John Dory, mussels, oysters, *pollack, salmon*, sea bass, *sea trout*

Foods in season

Foods in *italics* are foods from the UK at the peak of their season.

These tiny dumplings are delicious as a starter on their own or could be turned into a main course with, perhaps, a Bolognese, tuna fish or tomato and mushroom sauce. They make a nice change from the more usual all-potato ones. The trick is to dry the veg in the pan before mashing. If too wet, the dough won't be firm enough to shape.

Swede and potato gnocchi with melted butter and Parmesan

Serves 4

½ small swede, diced
2 large potatoes, diced
350 g plain flour
1 egg, beaten
Salt and freshly ground black
  pepper
75 g butter, melted
50 g Parmesan cheese, freshly
  grated

1 Cook the swede and potatoes together for about 10 minutes or until really tender. Drain thoroughly, return to the pan and heat gently to dry them out. Mash thoroughly.

2 Work in the flour, egg and a little salt and pepper to form a firm dough.

3 Knead gently on a lightly floured surface and then divide the mixture in half. Roll each piece to a sausage shape and cut into walnut-sized pieces. Roll into oval shapes.

4 Bring a large pan of lightly salted water to the boil. Drop the gnocchi into the pan and cook until they rise to the surface.

5 Remove from the pan with a draining spoon and drain on kitchen paper then transfer to warm individual serving dishes. Drizzle the melted butter over and sprinkle with Parmesan. Serve straight away.

This is the ideal vegetarian starter or meal: crisp pastry, creamy vegetable filling and a sweet onion marmalade to complement it. The onion marmalade goes well with grilled steaks or chops, too, and tastes good with cheese and French bread instead of chutney. For a main course, you might like to serve some potatoes and a side salad.

Carrot, watercress and cream cheese strudel with red onion

1 Melt the butter. Add the onions and fry, stirring, for 3 minutes.

2 Add the sugar and continue to fry for 5 minutes until caramelised.

3 Add the juice and vinegar, bring to the boil, reduce the heat and simmer for 1–2 minutes until thick. Remove from the heat.

4 Cook the carrots in boiling, lightly salted water for about 6 minutes until tender. Drain and mash well in a bowl.

5 Add the watercress, cream cheese, caraway seeds and some salt and pepper and mix well.

6 Brush four sheets of filo with oil and put another one on top of each. Brush again and put another sheet on top of each. Spoon the cheese mixture on top and spread out gently, not quite to the edges. Fold in the side edges then roll up not too tightly.

7 Transfer to an oiled baking sheet with the edge of the rolls underneath. Brush with a little more oil. Bake in a preheated oven at 220°C/gas 7/fan oven 200°C for about 20 minutes until golden and crisp.

8 Cool slightly then cut each strudel into three pieces, arrange on warm plates and put a spoonful of the onion marmalade to one side of each. Garnish each with a small sprig of watercress.

Serves 4–6

25 g butter
3 red onions, thinly sliced
1 tbsp demerara sugar
5 tbsp pure orange juice
2 tbsp balsamic vinegar
For the strudel:
4 carrots, scrubbed or peeled and thinly sliced
1 bunch of watercress, chopped, reserving 4–6 small sprigs for garnishing
225 g cream cheese
1 tbsp caraway seeds
Salt and freshly ground black pepper
12 sheets of filo pastry
2 tbsp olive oil

You must make sure the salmon is very fresh as it's served raw. Don't be put off by that – the flavour is absolutely superb. The fish is marinated in oil and mild white balsamic condiment with some fresh dill and then cut into very thin slices to serve with a sweet herby mayonnaise and crisp peppery radishes.

Salmon carpaccio with honey-dill mayonnaise and fresh radishes

Serves 4

450 g very fresh, thick, middle
   salmon fillet
4 tbsp olive oil
1 tbsp white balsamic condiment
1 bay leaf, broken into 4 pieces
1 sprig of fresh dill
1 shallot, thinly sliced
For the mayonnaise:
6 tbsp mayonnaise
2 tbsp chopped fresh dill
1 tsp Dijon mustard
2 tsp clear honey
1 tsp lemon juice
Small sprigs of dill and a bunch of
   radishes, for garnishing
To serve:
French bread

1 Remove the skin and any bones from the fish. Place the fish in a shallow container, just large enough to take it. Whisk the oil and balsamic condiment together and pour over. Turn to coat in the marinade. Add the broken bay leaf, dill and shallot slices. Cover and leave to marinate for 2 hours.

2 Lift out of the marinade and wrap tightly in clingfilm. Reserve the marinade. Freeze the fish for 1 hour to firm.

3 Meanwhile, mix the mayonnaise with the dill, mustard and honey. Whisk in the lemon juice and 1 tbsp of the marinade. Spoon into individual serving pots.

4 Remove the salmon from the freezer and cut into thin slices with a very sharp knife, slicing downwards into strips.

5 Arrange on four plates with a pot or a spoonful of mayonnaise on each. Top and tail the radishes and put a small cluster on each plate. Garnish each with a sprig of dill and serve with French bread.

Cooking the fish in spiced yoghurt makes it beautifully moist and tender. It's then tossed in cooked basmati rice, flavoured with mushrooms, onions, peas and chopped fresh coriander and garnished with currants and desiccated coconut. It's a complete meal with just a few little side dishes to add contrast and colour.

Pollack biryani with mushrooms, peas and coconut

1 Cook the basmati rice in plenty of boiling, lightly salted water for 10 minutes until just tender, adding the peas half way through cooking. Drain thoroughly in a colander and keep warm.

2 Meanwhile, fry the onions in the oil for 3 minutes, stirring, until lightly golden.

3 Add the mushrooms and spices and fry, stirring, for 1 minute.

4 Add the yoghurt, a little salt and pepper and the coriander and stir well. Add the fish, stir to coat in the yoghurt mixture, bring to the boil, reduce the heat and simmer, stirring very gently once or twice, for 5–7 minutes until the fish is bathed in sauce (the mixture will curdle first). Taste and re-season if necessary.

5 Add the rice. Stir very gently but thoroughly to mix.

6 Pile on to warm plates. Sprinkle with the currants and coconut and garnish each with a lemon wedge. Serve with sliced bananas, onions, cucumber and tomatoes.

Serves 4

350 g basmati rice
50 g frozen peas
1 tbsp sunflower oil
2 onions, sliced
100 g button mushrooms, quartered
1 tbsp mild curry paste
1 tsp ground turmeric
1 tsp grated fresh root ginger
120 ml plain yoghurt
Salt and freshly ground black pepper
1 tbsp chopped fresh coriander
4 pollack fillets, skinned and cubed
2 tbsp currants
2 tbsp desiccated coconut
Lemon wedges, for garnishing
To serve:
Sliced banana, tossed in lemon juice, sliced onions, cucumber and tomatoes

I am a great believer in animal welfare so suggest you at least look for outdoor-reared pork where the animals are allowed to roam free and have little metal huts to sleep and shelter in. Fillet is a good buy because there's virtually no waste and, when sliced and beaten out flat, a little goes a long way.

Pork fillet with orange gravy and garlic sautéed potatoes

Serves 4

350 g pork fillet, cut into 12 slices
Olive oil
50 g butter
4 large potatoes, diced
2 garlic cloves, halved
Finely grated zest and juice of
    1 orange
150 ml chicken or pork stock,
    ideally fresh or made with
    ½ stock cube
½ tsp dried mixed herbs
Salt and freshly ground black
    pepper
To serve:
Purple sprouting broccoli

1 Put the slices of pork in a plastic bag a few at a time and beat with a meat mallet or rolling pin to flatten.

2 Pour enough olive oil into a frying pan to come 5 mm/¼ in up the sides. Add half the butter. Heat until the butter melts and bubbles, stir then add the potatoes and garlic. Fry, turning occasionally, for about 6–8 minutes until golden all over and cooked through. Drain on kitchen paper, discard the garlic halves and keep warm.

3 Meanwhile, heat the remaining butter with 1 tbsp of olive oil in a separate pan. Fry the pork for about 1–2 minutes on each side until golden and cooked through. Transfer to a plate and keep warm.

4 Add the orange zest and juice, the stock and herbs to the pan juices. Bring to the boil and boil rapidly, scraping up any sediment until reduced. Season to taste.

5 Pile the potatoes on to four warm plates. Lay the pork slices to one side and spoon the orange gravy over. Serve with purple sprouting broccoli.

Make sure you buy free-range birds both for flavour as well as welfare. I like corn-fed chickens but the choice is yours. Here the breasts are cooked quickly with spring greens, onions, garlic, fresh root ginger and the bamboo shoots to add an authentic Oriental flavour.

Chicken and spring green stir-fry with bamboo shoots

1 Heat the oils in a wok or large frying pan. Add the chicken and stir-fry for 2 minutes.

2 Add the greens, onions and garlic and stir-fry for 4 minutes.

3 Add the remaining ingredients except the noodles. Stir-fry for a further 2 minutes.

4 Meanwhile, cook the noodles according to the packet directions. Drain.

5 Put the noodles into four warm bowls. Top with the stir-fry and serve.

Serves 4

2 tbsp sunflower oil
1 tsp sesame oil
4 skinless chicken breasts, cut into thin strips
350 g spring greens, finely shredded, discarding any thick stalks
2 onions, thinly sliced
2 garlic cloves, crushed
1 tsp grated fresh root ginger
225 g can of bamboo shoots, drained
3 tbsp soy sauce
2 tbsp apple juice
225 g rice noodles

Purple sprouting broccoli is appearing more and more in the shops as well as farmers' markets. It's a good crop to grow as, it seems, the more you cut the more it grows! Choose thin, tender stems and small, tight heads. Here it's lightly cooked as a side dish and bathed in butter and olive oil, flavoured with spring onions and almonds.

Purple sprouting broccoli with spring onions and almonds

Serves 4

250 g purple sprouting broccoli
25 g butter
45 ml olive oil
1 bunch of spring onions, chopped
25 g flaked almonds
1 tbsp chopped fresh parsley

1 Trim the stalks of the broccoli and separate into individual heads and stalks, if necessary. Cut any large ones in half lengthways.

2 Cook in boiling, lightly salted water, or steam for 4–6 minutes until just tender but still with some 'bite'. Drain, if cooked in water. Transfer to a serving dish.

3 Heat the butter and oil in a frying pan. Add the spring onions and almonds and fry, stirring, just until the almonds turn golden. Throw in the parsley. Quickly spoon over the broccoli and serve with any meat, fish or poultry.

Photograph opposite:
Salmon carpaccio with honey-dill
mayonnaise and fresh radishes
(see page 44)

This is everyone's favourite side dish from the Chinese restaurant but it's so easy to cook at home! The knack is to shred the greens very finely, have the oil very hot, use a frying basket and to cook them in very small batches, very quickly. If you cook too many at once, the temperature of the oil drops and the results will be soggy.

Crispy spring green seaweed with five-spice

1 Roll up the greens and cut in as fine shreds as you can using sharp scissors.

2 Heat some oil for deep-frying until a cube of day-old bread browns in 30 seconds.

3 Fry the greens in small batches for 30 seconds until crispy but still bright green. Drain on kitchen paper and tip into a bowl. Re-heat the oil before each batch.

4 Mix the salt and five-spice powder together and sprinkle over the greens. Toss well and serve.

Serves 4

300 g spring greens
Groundnut or corn oil for frying
½ tsp salt
½ tsp Chinese five-spice powder

Photograph opposite:
Honey-glazed spring lamb cutlets
with minted peas and potatoes
(see page 84)

I'm a great fan of ordinary crème brulée and wasn't sure how I'd enjoy a fruity one. However, I'm delighted that this pale pink, velvety concoction brings out the full flavour of the fruit but still has a lovely creamy aftertaste, and the caramelised crunch on top rounds it off beautifully.

Pink rhubarb in rosé crème brulée

Serves 4

450 g forced rhubarb, trimmed and
   cut in short lengths
150 ml rosé wine
75 g granulated sugar
300 ml double cream
4 eggs
A few drops of cochineal (optional)
75 g caster sugar

1 Put the rhubarb in a saucepan with the wine and sugar. Bring to the boil, reduce the heat, part-cover and simmer gently until the rhubarb is really tender, about 10 minutes.

2 Tip into a blender or food processor and run the machine until smooth.

3 Cool slightly then blend in the cream and the eggs. Add a few drops of cochineal, if liked.

4 Pour into six ramekin dishes. Stand the dishes in a roasting tin with enough hot water to come half-way up the sides of the dishes. Cook in a preheated oven at 160°C/gas 3/fan oven 145°C for about 30 minutes until set.

5 Remove from the roasting tin, leave to cool, then chill.

6 Cover the tops with caster sugar. Either use a blow torch or place the dishes under a preheated grill, as near the heat source as possible, until the sugar has caramelised. Serve within an hour.

You can buy pineapples pretty much all year round but they are at their best right now – sweet and juicy. Choose one that smells fruity and is golden yellow in colour. Avoid any that are green, deep orange or very soft. Try this recipe with vanilla or coffee ice-cream instead of crème fraîche if you prefer.

Golden glazed pineapple with rum and butter sauce

1 Cut off the green top and the base from the pineapple then cut into four slices.

2 Cut the rind off each slice and cut out the core if tough.

3 Melt half the butter in a large frying pan. Sprinkle the pineapple with 4 tsp of the sugar and add to the pan, sugar-side down. Fry for 2 minutes. Sprinkle with a further 4 tsp of the sugar and turn the pineapple over. Fry again until brown. Transfer to warm plates with a draining spoon.

4 Add the remaining butter and sugar to the pan over a gentle heat and stir until melted. Add the rum and fruit juice and boil rapidly, stirring until slightly thickened.

5 Spoon over the pineapple and serve with crème fraîche.

Serves 4

1 small ripe pineapple
50 g butter
75 g demerara sugar
2 tbsp rum
2 tbsp pineapple or orange juice
To serve:
Crème fraîche

Winter-stored crops are pretty much over now but the main spring crops are only just beginning. **Lettuces** and **watercress** are good and **spinach** should be cropping well. **Spring onions** and **cauliflowers** are excellent this month, as is **purple sprouting broccoli**. **Poussins** are now available all year but were traditionally a spring bird and are particularly good around now. **Rhubarb**, technically a vegetable, is still around this month and you may find the last of the stored apples and pears (but they are by no means at their peak). Of imported fruit, **kiwis** and **mangoes** are my favourites at this time of year. The first **English lamb** should be ready this month if the climate is mild.

April

Vegetables

Broccoli, cabbages (green), *carrots, cauliflowers, garlic,* horseradish, Jersey Royal new potatoes, *lettuces,* morel mushrooms, *purple sprouting broccoli, radishes,* rhubarb, rocket, *sorrel, spinach, spring greens, spring onions, watercress*

Fruit and nuts

Avocados (Fuerte and Hass), bananas, kiwi fruit, loquats, mangoes, muscat grapes

Meat, poultry and game

Lamb, *poussins,* rabbit, *wood pigeon*

Fish and seafood

Brown shrimps, cockles, cod, *crabs,* Dublin Bay prawns (scampi), halibut, John Dory, *salmon,* sea bass, *sea trout*

Foods in season

Foods in *italics* are foods from the UK at the peak of their season.

This smooth, rich soup is delicious served with some crusty bread and followed by some cold ham, pickles and a side salad, for a perfect, simple meal. For a touch of added elegance, add a swirl of double cream to each bowl before sprinkling with parsley.

Velvety cauliflower and Cheddar cheese soup

Serves 4

15 g butter
1 onion, chopped
1 small cauliflower, cut in small florets, greens and thick stump discarded
1 large potato, diced
600 ml vegetable stock, ideally fresh or made with 1 stock cube
1 bouquet garni sachet
Salt and freshly ground black pepper
100 g Cheddar cheese, grated
300 ml milk
1 tbsp chopped fresh parsley, for garnishing

1 Melt the butter in a saucepan. Add the onion and fry, stirring, for 2 minutes until softened but not browned.

2 Add the cauliflower, potato, stock, bouquet garni sachet and a little salt and pepper. Bring to the boil, reduce the heat, part-cover and simmer for 20 minutes until the vegetables are really tender. Discard the bouquet garni.

3 Tip into a blender or food processor and run the machine until smooth.

4 Return to the pan and stir in the cheese and milk. Heat gently, stirring, until the cheese melts. Taste and re-season if necessary.

5 Ladle into warm bowls and garnish with chopped parsley.

This salad of tender, young, home-grown spinach, spring onions and sun-blushed tomatoes, interspersed with creamy just-ripe avocado and silvery marinated anchovies, celebrates the delights of fusion food. It's dressed in a light vinaigrette, flavoured with fresh thyme.

Spinach and avocado salad with anchovies and soft-boiled eggs

1 Cut the bread into cubes. Heat 3 tbsp of the oil in a frying pan and fry the ciabatta, tossing until golden. Drain on kitchen paper.

2 Put the eggs in a small saucepan and just cover with cold water. Bring to the boil and boil for exactly 3½ minutes. Transfer the eggs immediately to a bowl of cold water.

3 Pile the spinach into four large salad bowls.

4 Halve, stone, peel and dice the avocados and toss in the lemon juice. Add to the spinach with the spring onions, sun-blushed tomatoes and anchovies.

5 Whisk the remaining oil with the balsamic vinegar, the thyme, a pinch of salt and a good grinding of pepper. Pour over the salads and toss gently.

6 Carefully shell the eggs. Put one on top of each salad and cut through almost in half so the lovely runny yolk trickles out.

7 Sprinkle with chopped parsley and serve straight away.

Serves 4

4 slices of ciabatta bread
5 tbsp olive oil
4 eggs
100 g baby leaf spinach
2 avocados
2 tsp lemon juice
4 spring onions, chopped
8 sun-blushed tomatoes, drained and halved
100 g marinated anchovies, drained
1½ tbsp balsamic vinegar
1 tbsp chopped fresh thyme
Salt and freshly ground black pepper
1 tbsp chopped fresh parsley

This is a stunning, elegant way of making individual pies without the pastry becoming soggy. Broccoli is in season but not at its peak but it's still worth using in this dish. The combination with the salmon is just perfect. You could use the same idea with smoked haddock and baby broad beans in June.

Fresh salmon and broccoli cream puff layers

Serves 4

1 sheet of frozen, ready-rolled puff pastry, just thawed
1 egg, beaten
225 g broccoli, cut in tiny florets
300 ml milk
1 bay leaf
4 black peppercorns
½ onion, sliced
450 g fresh salmon, skinned
A good knob of butter
5 tbsp plain flour
2 tbsp double cream
Salt and freshly ground black pepper
A squeeze of lemon juice
Watercress, for garnishing
To serve:
Jersey Royal new potatoes and peas

1 Cut the sheet of pastry in half lengthways then cut across in quarters to make eight equal rectangles.

2 Place on a dampened baking sheet (use two if necessary). Score four of the sheets in a criss-cross pattern with a sharp knife but don't cut right through. Brush all the rectangles with beaten egg. Bake in a preheated oven at 220°C/gas 7/fan oven 200°C for about 15–20 minutes until risen and golden brown.

3 Meanwhile, steam or cook the broccoli in a little lightly salted boiling water for 3–4 minutes until just tender but still with some texture. Drain, if necessary.

4 Put the milk, bay leaf, peppercorns and onion in a frying pan. Bring to the boil.

5 Add the salmon, cover and poach over a gentle heat for 8–10 minutes until the fish flakes easily.

6 Lift out carefully and flake with a fork. Discard the skin and any remaining bones.

7 Melt the butter in a large saucepan and stir in the flour. Remove from the heat. Strain the cooking milk and whisk into the butter and flour. Season. Return to the heat, bring to the boil and cook for 2 minutes, stirring until thick and smooth.

8   Add the cream, fish and broccoli. Season to taste with salt and pepper and sharpen with a squeeze of lemon juice.

9   Put the four unscored pastry rectangles on four warm plates. Spoon the salmon and broccoli mixture over, then lay the scored sheets on top at a jaunty angle.

10 Garnish with watercress and serve with Jersey Royal potatoes and peas.

Potted shrimps or prawns

This is a little spring favourite of mine. Melt 225 g unsalted butter and stir in 225 g cooked peeled shrimps or prawns. Heat gently, stirring, for 2 minutes but don't boil or they'll go rubbery. Add ¼ tsp ground mace, a pinch of salt, some freshly ground black pepper and a few drops of Tabasco sauce. Pack into 4 small pots and cover with a thin layer of extra melted unsalted butter. Chill until firm. Serve with hot toast or crusty wholemeal bread.

Shrimps are fiddly to peel but the flavour is fantastic. If you can't find any, you can use prawns instead. If you have homemade fish or chicken stock, do use it instead of the stock cubes, the resulting flavour will be worth it! I like to serve a watercress salad with a lemon dressing as an accompaniment.

Brown shrimp risotto with vermouth and Parmesan

Serves 4

700 g brown shrimps
60 g unsalted butter
1 onion, chopped
1 small garlic clove, crushed
1.2 litres fish or chicken stock,
    ideally fresh or made with
    2 stock cubes
1 bay leaf
4 shallots, finely chopped
350 g risotto rice
4 tbsp dry vermouth
40 g Parmesan cheese, freshly
    grated
Salt and freshly ground black
    pepper
2 tbsp chopped fresh parsley

1 Peel the shrimps, reserving the shells.

2 Melt 15 g of the butter in a large pan. Add the onion and fry, stirring, for 2 minutes. Add the garlic, stock, bay leaf and shrimp shells. Bring to the boil, part-cover and simmer over a moderate heat for 15 minutes. Strain, pressing the shells against the sieve with the back of a spoon to extract all the flavour. Return the stock to the pan and keep hot over a low heat.

3 Melt 25 g of the remaining butter in a separate saucepan. Add the shallots and fry gently, stirring, for 2 minutes until softened but not browned. Add the rice and stir until every grain is glistening with butter.

4 Add the vermouth and bubble until it's been absorbed, stirring. Add 2 ladlefuls of stock and again allow to bubble over a very gentle heat until the stock has been absorbed, stirring all the time. Keep adding the stock, two ladlefuls at a time, stirring continuously. After 15 minutes, add the shrimps and continue to add the last of the stock. The whole thing should take about 20 minutes until all the stock is used and the risotto is creamy but the rice still has some 'bite'.

5 Stir in half the cheese and the remaining butter.

6 Serve in warm soup plates with the rest of the Parmesan and the parsley sprinkled over.

As I've said before, poussins – or spring chicken – are available all year but are still the perfect food for spring. Here they are teamed with flavoursome woodland morel mushrooms, earthy Jersey Royals and finely shredded fresh spring greens for a complete dish with rustic charm that's also elegant enough for a dinner party.

Pan-roasted spring chicken with morels and spring greens

1 Heat half the oil and half the butter in a wok or large frying pan. Add the shallots and potatoes and fry, stirring, until golden all over. Remove from the pan.

2 Heat the remaining oil and butter in the pan and brown the poussins on both sides.

3 Return the potatoes and shallots to the pan and add the mushrooms and some salt and pepper. Cover and cook over a gentle heat for 20 minutes.

4 Add the greens. Pour the stock around, sprinkle the garlic and parsley over the top, re-cover and cook for 10 minutes.

5 Transfer the chicken and vegetables to four warm plates and keep them warm.

6 Boil the pan juices to reduce slightly. Taste and re-season if necessary. Spoon over the chicken and serve hot with French bread.

Serves 4

2 tbsp olive oil
25 g butter
12 shallots, peeled but left whole
450 g Jersey Royals, scrubbed and cut in pieces if large
2 poussins, halved
175 g morel mushrooms
Salt and freshly ground black pepper
1 head of spring greens, finely shredded, discarding the thick stalk
250 ml chicken stock, ideally fresh or made with $1/2$ stock cube
2 garlic cloves, finely chopped
3 tbsp chopped fresh parsley
To serve:
French bread

Meat, game and poultry   **59**

Rabbit is very like chicken to eat – lean, tender and subtle in flavour. I love it cooked this way with carrots and button mushrooms in a rich, creamy, sherried sauce, topped with a layer of crisp, flaky, buttery pastry. Incidentally, this type of pastry is simple and satisfying to make and is a lovely change from the bought puff variety.

Butter-crust rabbit pie with carrots, mushrooms and sherry

Serves 4

For the flaky pastry:
225 g plain flour
A good pinch of salt
175 g cold butter, cut into pieces
About 8 tbsp cold water to mix
For the filling:
1 oven-ready rabbit
2 onions, chopped
4 carrots, sliced
100 g button mushrooms, sliced
500 ml water
3 tbsp dry sherry
½ tsp dried mixed herbs
Salt and freshly ground black
    pepper
4 tbsp plain flour
8 tbsp milk
4 tbsp single cream, plus extra for
    glazing
2 tbsp chopped fresh parsley
To serve:
Roasted baby potatoes and spinach

1 Sift the flour and salt into a bowl. Add 50 g of the butter and rub in with the fingertips until it resembles breadcrumbs.

2 Add the remaining butter. Using a knife, mix in the water to form a lumpy dough, finally drawing the mixture into a rough ball with the fingers.

3 Turn out on to a lightly floured surface. Roll the dough out to a rough rectangle then fold the top third down and the bottom third up over it. Press the edges together then give the dough a quarter turn. Repeat the rolling and folding three times. Wrap in clingfilm, then chill.

4 Cut the rabbit into pieces. Place in a large pan with the onions, carrots, mushrooms, water, sherry, herbs and a little salt and pepper. Bring to the boil, reduce the heat and simmer gently for about 45 minutes or until tender.

5 Remove from the heat. Lift out the rabbit with a draining spoon. When cool enough to handle, take all the meat off the bones and cut into neat pieces.

6 Blend the flour with the milk and stir into the stock and vegetables. Bring to the boil, stirring until thickened. Stir in the cream and parsley. Return the rabbit to the sauce. Taste and re-season.

7 Turn the mixture into a 1.2 litre pie dish. Put a pie funnel in the centre.

8 Roll and fold the pastry once more, then roll out to slightly larger than the pie dish. Cut a strip off all round. Dampen the rim of the pie dish and lay the strip of pastry on the rim. Put the pastry on top, making a small cross-cut in the centre. Press all round the edge, trim and knock up with the back of a knife. Flute the edge.

9 Brush the pastry with a little single cream. Make leaves out of pastry trimmings and place in the centre. Brush again.

10 Place the pie on a baking sheet and bake in a preheated oven at 220°C/gas 7/fan oven 200°C for 20 minutes until the pastry is risen and golden. Turn down the heat to 180°C/gas 4/fan oven 160°C and cook for a further 10 minutes. Serve hot with roasted baby potatoes and spinach.

Quick crunchy lamb cutlets

This is another great recipe for this time of year, and it's particularly good if you're short of time. It's good with pork chops or chicken legs, too. Trim the ends of some lamb cutlet bones. Dip them in seasoned flour, then beaten egg, then any dry breadcrumb-based stuffing mix like parsley, thyme and lemon, sage and onion or country-style. Repeat the dipping and coating, then chill, if you have time, to firm up the coating. Fry in a little hot oil and butter for 3–5 minutes each side until golden and crunchy (or 6–8 minutes for pork or chicken). Drain on kitchen paper and serve hot or cold.

Cauliflower has long been served bathed in a cheese sauce, and very good that is, too. But I like to enjoy the full flavour of the cauliflower, mingled with the sweet but sharp taste of tomato in an easy-to-make, creamy béchamel sauce. This is equally good with broccoli. It tastes great with any roasted or grilled meat.

Cauliflower cream with passata and basil

Serves 4

1 small cauliflower, cut in small
   florets
20 g plain flour
200 ml milk
A good knob of butter
1 bay leaf
6 tbsp single cream
Salt and freshly ground black
   pepper
175 ml passata
½ tsp dried basil

1 Cook the cauliflower in a small amount of boiling, lightly salted water for about 4 minutes until just tender but still with some 'bite'. Drain and turn into a flameproof serving dish.

2 Whisk the flour and milk together in a saucepan. Add the butter and bay leaf. Bring to the boil, whisking all the time, until thick. Whisk in the cream.

3 Season to taste and discard the bay leaf.

4 Spoon the passata over the cauliflower and sprinkle with the basil.

5 Pour the sauce over and glaze under a preheated grill for 2–3 minutes until lightly coloured on top. Serve hot.

The unmistakable, earthy flavour of Jersey Royal potatoes makes them the kings of the crop. They can be scraped very easily or simply scrubbed in cold water before cooking. They are divine plainly boiled or steamed, but they are magical bathed in melted unsalted butter with fresh mint and garlic, especially with grills.

Jersey Royals with fresh mint and garlic butter

1   Boil the potatoes in lightly salted water for about 10 minutes or until tender. Drain and return to the pan.

2   Add a good grinding of black pepper, the butter, mint and garlic. Toss over a gentle heat until the butter has melted and coats the potatoes. Serve hot.

Serves 4

450 g Jersey Royal new potatoes, scraped
Salt and freshly ground black pepper
50 g unsalted butter
2 tbsp chopped fresh mint
1 garlic clove, crushed

If you like the fragrant flavour of rosewater, try stirring a tablespoonful into the pudding before spooning over the mango sauce. At other times of the year, you could try making a raspberry, strawberry or plum sauce instead of using mangoes. The amount of icing sugar you use will depend on your taste.

Rice pudding with fresh mango sauce

Serves 4

50 g pudding rice
410 g can of evaporated milk
40 g caster sugar
For the sauce:
1 ripe mango
2 tsp lemon or lime juice
2 tbsp icing sugar

1 Put the rice in a heavy-based saucepan with the evaporated milk. Fill the empty can with water and tip into the pan as well.

2 Stir in the sugar. Bring to the boil, stirring. Reduce the heat and simmer gently for 50 minutes until the rice is tender and creamy, stirring occasionally.

3 Meanwhile, peel the mango and cut all the flesh off the stone. Place in a blender or food processor with the lemon or lime juice and the icing sugar. Run the machine until smooth. Tip into a small saucepan and heat through, stirring.

4 Spoon the rice into four serving dishes. Swirl the mango sauce over and serve hot.

British fruits are not in season this month but avocados are really good right now. Everybody thinks of them as a savoury food – and a vegetable to boot. But they are a fruit and they taste wonderful for dessert. Eat these mousses on the day they are made as they will discolour after a while.

Sweet avocado mousse in its shell

1 Put the gelatine in a small bowl with the water. Leave to soften for 5 minutes then stand the bowl in a pan of hot water and heat, stirring, until the gelatine has completely dissolved.

2 Halve the avocados, discard the stones and gently scoop the flesh into a blender or food processor, taking care not to damage the skins. Add the lemon juice and icing sugar and blend until smooth. Add the gelatine and blend again. Turn the mixture into a bowl.

3 Whisk the egg white until stiff and the cream until it holds soft peaks.

4 Add about two-thirds of the cream to the avocado mixture and fold in with a metal spoon. Lastly fold in the egg white.

5 Spoon the mixture into the avocado shells, then chill until set. Spread the remaining cream over and decorate with angelica 'leaves' and crystallised violets or rose petals.

Serves 4

2 tsp powdered gelatine
3 tbsp water
2 just-ripe avocados
1½ tbsp lemon juice
50 g icing sugar, sifted
1 egg white
250 ml double cream
4 angelica 'leaves' and crystallised violets or rose petals

When **English asparagus** arrives, I really feel summer is on the way. You'll find the first **baby broad beans**, fabulous **Jersey Royals**, fresh greens in the form of **spinach, sorrel, watercress** and **rocket** and unusual herbs like **lovage** are around. It's also the brief season of **elderflowers** – enjoy them as fritters, use them to flavour syrups or make **elderflower fizz**. Just put about 20 heads of elderflowers in a sterilised bucket with 2.2 litres of water, 350 g granulated sugar, the thinly pared zest and juice of 1 small lemon and 4 tsp cider vinegar. Stir well to dissolve the sugar, cover with a lid or a clean cloth and leave to stand for 24 hours. Strain and pour into sterilised screw-topped bottles. Screw on the tops firmly and leave for about 10 days. Test after five days and release a little gas, so the bottles don't explode.

May

Vegetables

Asparagus, broad beans, broccoli, *carrots, cauliflowers, cucumbers, globe artichokes, Jersey Royal new potatoes, lettuces, lovage*, new potatoes, peas, *radishes*, rhubarb, *rocket, sorrel, spinach*, spring onions, *watercress*

Fruit and nuts

Avocados (Fuerte and Hass), *cherry tomatoes*, cherries, *elderflowers*, kiwi fruit lychees, mangoes

Meat, poultry and game

Lamb, *wood pigeon*

Fish and seafood

Bream, *brown shrimps*, cod, *crabs, crayfish*, Dover sole, *Dublin Bay prawns (scampi)*, halibut, John Dory, *pollack*, prawns, river trout (brown, rainbow), *salmon*, sea bass, *sea trout*

Foods in season

Foods in *italics* are foods from the UK at the peak of their season.

Manchego cheese has a sweet, salty flavour and is a more subtle accompaniment to asparagus and salmon than the more usual Parmesan. The modern classic way of serving the asparagus is just plain griddled with melted butter or olive oil but this makes a gorgeous, more decadent starter.

Griddled asparagus with smoked salmon curls

Serves 4

4 thin slices of smoked salmon
24 asparagus spears
4 tbsp olive oil
4 tsp balsamic vinegar
50 g Manchego cheese, flaked with
　a potato peeler
Freshly ground black pepper

1　Roll up each slice of salmon and cut into thin strips.

2　Trim about 2.5 cm off the bottom of each asparagus stalk. Toss the spears in a little of the olive oil.

3　Cook in an electric griddle for 2–3 minutes until just tender or for 4–6 minutes in a hot griddle pan, turning once.

4　Lay the asparagus on serving plates. Trickle with the olive oil and balsamic vinegar. Scatter the salmon curls and cheese flakes over and add a good grinding of black pepper.

You can make the dough in a bread machine on the dough programme then continue from step 4. I love black pudding, but if you prefer you could use some cooked ham or some continental sausage like chorizo or salami cut or torn into small pieces. The important thing is the contrast in flavours.

Spinach, egg, black pudding and Blue Vinney pizza

1 Mix the flour with the salt and sugar in a bowl. Add the oil and yeast and mix with the water to form a soft but not sticky dough. Knead for 5 minutes on a lightly floured surface, or use a food processor. Cover with oiled clingfilm and leave in a warm place for 45 minutes until doubled in bulk.

2 Re-knead the dough, divide into four equal pieces and shape into four rounds or ovals, about 18 cm/7 in diameter. Place on two oiled baking sheets. Spread with the tomato purée, cover lightly with oiled clingfilm and leave in a warm place.

3 Wash the spinach, shake off the excess water then put in a saucepan. Cover and cook for 5 minutes. Drain, then chop.

4 Sprinkle the tomato purée with the oregano. Scatter the spinach over (it will be in small clumps). Scatter the blue cheese over then add small spoonfuls of the white soft cheese at intervals. Finally scatter the black pudding over.

5 Bake in a preheated oven at 220°C/gas 7/fan oven 200°C for 10–15 minutes until just beginning to turn brown at the edges. Turn the baking sheets round.

6 Make a well in the centre of each pizza and break an egg into it. Scatter the Mozzarella and basil over and plenty of pepper. Return to the oven for 10 minutes until the eggs are just set, the edges are browned and the cheese has melted.

Serves 4

For the dough:
350 g white bread flour
1 tsp salt
1 tsp caster sugar
2 tbsp olive oil, plus extra for drizzling
2 tsp easy-blend dried yeast
250 ml hand-hot water

For the topping:
4 tbsp tomato purée
350 g spinach
$\frac{1}{2}$ tsp dried oregano
100 g Blue Vinney (or other blue cheese), crumbled
100 g white soft cheese
4 thick slices of black pudding, cut into small pieces
4 eggs
100 g Mozzarella, grated
A few torn fresh basil leaves
Freshly ground black pepper

Prawns are in season and, although not at their absolute best this month, they are still worth using. However, you could use freshwater crayfish, if you can get them, or Dublin Bay prawns instead if you like. The result is a very modern lasagne that cooks in just a few minutes instead of the more usual baked layered dish.

Garlic, prawn and lasagne layers with Mascarpone

Serves 4

For the sauce:
1 tbsp olive oil
1 onion, finely chopped
450 g tomatoes, skinned and chopped
1 tbsp tomato purée
½ tsp caster sugar
1 tsp chopped fresh thyme
Salt and freshly ground black pepper
For the filling:
8 fresh or dried green lasagne sheets
2 tbsp olive oil
1 garlic clove, crushed
450 g raw peeled prawns
2 tbsp chopped fresh parsley
100 g Mascarpone cheese
75 g Cheddar cheese, grated
To serve:
A green salad

1 Make the sauce. Heat the oil in a saucepan. Add the onion and fry, stirring, for 2 minutes. Add the tomatoes, purée, sugar, thyme and some salt and pepper. Bring to the boil, stirring, reduce the heat and simmer for 5 minutes until pulpy.

2 Cook the lasagne sheets in boiling water for about 3 minutes for fresh, 8 minutes for dried, until tender. Drain in a colander, rinse with cold water and separate out so they don't stick together.

3 Heat the oil in a frying pan. Add the garlic and prawns and fry quickly, stirring, for 2 minutes until the prawns are pink. Throw in the parsley.

4 Put a sheet of lasagne on each of four shallow flameproof dishes. Spread with the Mascarpone cheese.

5 Spoon the garlic prawns on top and lay the other sheets of lasagne over. Spoon the tomato sauce over, sprinkle with the grated cheese and flash under a preheated grill for 3–4 minutes until piping hot.

6 Serve with a green salad.

You can use any fish fillets in season for this dish and try it with oysters, mussels or prawns instead of the scampi (which aren't easy to come by). I adore tempura and you can make a vegetable one too, using pieces of courgette, pepper and onions and some whole button mushrooms and mangetout instead of the fish.

Sea trout and scampi tempura with rice wine dipping sauce

1 Mix the dipping sauce ingredients together and pour into four small serving dishes.

2 Sift 125 g of the flour and the salt into a bowl.

3 Beat the egg with the water.

4 Quickly beat into the flour to form a thickish batter.

5 Mix the remaining flour with a little salt and pepper. Heat the oil until a cube of day-old bread browns in 30 seconds. Dip the fish and scampi tails in the seasoned flour, then in the batter, drain off excess and deep-fry for about 2–3 minutes until crisp and golden. Drain on kitchen paper. Serve with the dipping sauce.

Serves 4

For the dipping sauce:
5 tbsp rice wine
5 tbsp soy sauce
1 spring onion, very finely chopped
1 garlic clove, crushed
For the tempura batter:
145 g plain flour
A pinch of salt
1 large egg
150 ml ice-cold sparkling mineral water
For the fish:
Salt and freshly ground black pepper
Oil for deep-frying
300 g sea trout fillets, skinned and cut into bite-sized pieces
200 g raw peeled Dublin Bay prawn (scampi) tails

Chicken livers are cheap, plentiful and extremely delicious. The trick is not to overcook them. They should always be lightly browned on the outside but still pink in the centre. Baby broad beans are perfect early in the season – small, pearly green and very tender. If lovage isn't available, use sage or rosemary instead.

Pan-fried chicken livers with broad beans and lovage

Serves 4

350 g wild rice mix
700 g broad beans, shelled
25 g butter
2 onions, finely chopped
1 garlic clove, crushed
500 g chicken livers, trimmed
2 tbsp chopped fresh lovage
Salt and freshly ground black
   pepper
4 tbsp dry vermouth
A little chopped parsley, for
   garnishing

1 Cook the wild rice mix according to the packet directions. Drain and keep warm.

2 Cook the broad beans in boiling, lightly salted water for about 8 minutes until just tender. Drain. When cool enough to handle, pop out of the skins, if liked.

3 Heat the butter in a large frying pan. Add the onion and fry for 3 minutes, stirring, until softened and lightly golden. Add the garlic, chicken livers, lovage and a little salt and pepper and fry, stirring, for 4 minutes.

4 Add the vermouth to the pan, bring to the boil and bubble for 30 seconds.

5 Add the broad beans and toss to coat in the pan juices. Heat through, stirring for a minute. Taste and re-season if necessary.

6 Spoon the rice on to warm plates and top with the livers and broad beans. Sprinkle with a little chopped parsley. Serve hot.

Photograph opposite:
Sesame chicken and nori wraps
with chilli and ginger sauce
(see page 108)

Pigeons are a bit fiddly because it really is only the breasts that are worth eating. You can casserole them whole until very tender but I, like many food writers, prefer to use the rest of the birds for a flavoursome stock to go with the breasts. This is also lovely with duck wing portions treated the same way.

Pigeon breasts with lychees and soy sauce

1 Cut the breasts off the pigeons, following the line of the rib cage. Remove the skin.

2 Break up the carcasses. Heat 1 tbsp of the oil in a large saucepan. Add the carcasses and brown all over.

3 Add the water, garlic, carrot and spring onion trimmings. Bring to the boil, reduce the heat, part-cover and simmer gently for 30 minutes. Strain into a measuring jug – you should have about 200 ml.

4 Chop the spring onions. Reserve a little for garnishing. Spread the pigeon breasts with the wasabi paste.

5 Heat the oil in a wok or large frying pan. Add the pigeon breasts and brown quickly on both sides. Remove from the pan. Add the spring onions and shiitake mushrooms and stir-fry for 2 minutes. Add the stock, the pigeon breasts, lychees and ginger and bring to the boil. Reduce the heat, cover and cook gently for 6 minutes. Lift the pigeon out of the pan again.

6 Blend the cornflour with the soy sauce. Stir into the pan. Bring to the boil, stirring until thickened.

7 Meanwhile, cook the noodles according to the packet directions. Drain and pile in warm bowls. Top with the pigeon and sauce and sprinkle with the reserved chopped spring onion.

Serves 4

4 pigeons
3 tbsp sunflower oil
600 ml water
1 garlic clove, crushed
1 carrot, chopped
1 bunch of spring onions, trimmed, reserving the trimmings
1½ tsp wasabi paste
100 g shiitake mushrooms, sliced
100 g fresh lychees, peeled, stoned and halved
½ tsp grated fresh root ginger
2 tsp cornflour
2 tbsp soy sauce
225 g fresh egg noodles

Photograph opposite:
Sizzling scallops with lime, fennel and fresh chilli oil
(see page 118)

This is a lovely main meal served with crusty bread but can also be served in half the quantity as a starter or a side dish to accompany fish, meat or poultry. Try it topped with some crisp fried bacon, too. It's another dish that benefits from using the early, baby broad beans. The older, more floury ones don't have such a delicate flavour.

Linguine with baby broad bean cream

Serves 4

700 g broad beans, shelled
400 g linguine
25 g butter
2 onions, finely chopped
1 vegetable stock cube
200 g crème fraîche
2 tbsp chopped fresh parsley
25 g Parmesan, freshly grated

1 Cook the broad beans in boiling, lightly salted water for about 8 minutes until tender. Drain, reserving 250 ml of the stock. When cool enough to handle, gently squeeze the beans out of their skins.

2 Cook the linguine according to the packet directions. Drain and return to the pan.

3 Meanwhile, melt the butter in a saucepan. Add the onion and fry, stirring, over a gentle heat for 3 minutes until softened not browned. Add the reserved stock and the stock cube, bring to the boil and boil rapidly for about 8 minutes until well reduced.

4 Stir in the crème fraîche, parsley and half the Parmesan. Add the broad beans.

5 Tip the bean mixture into the pasta and toss over a gentle heat until every strand is coated in the sauce. Pile on warm plates, sprinkle with the remaining Parmesan and serve.

Sherry vinegar makes a welcome change from balsamic in this pretty side-dish to serve with plain meat, fish or eggs. It has just the right amount of acidity to complement the tomatoes. Take care when cooking so the fruit doesn't detach itself from the vine. If one or two stray, just tuck them back by the vine when you dish up!

Glazed vine-ripened cherry tomatoes in sherry vinegar

1 Heat the oil in a large frying pan. Add the sprigs of tomatoes. Sprinkle with the sugar and fry, shaking the pan gently, for 1 minute. Pour over the vinegar and season lightly.

2 Fry gently for a further 2 minutes, tilting the pan and spooning the juices over the tomatoes until they are just tender but still holding their shape.

3 Transfer the tomatoes to plates and spoon the pan juices over.

Serves 4

2 tbsp olive oil
4 sprigs of cherry tomatoes on the vine, with 5–6 fruit to each sprig
1 tbsp soft light brown sugar
2 tbsp sherry vinegar
Salt and freshly ground black pepper

The flowers must be freshly picked to get the best flavour. You can just sprinkle the fritters with sugar if you don't want the sticky drizzle but if you're going to be decadent enough to eat batter then you may as well go the whole hog! This fritter batter is good with fresh pineapple, apples and bananas, too.

Elderflower fritters with honey lime drizzle

Serves 4

4 tbsp clear honey
Finely grated zest and juice of
 ½ lime
40 g plain flour
25 g cornflour
1 tsp baking powder
A pinch of salt
150 ml cold soda water
8 elderflower heads
Corn oil for deep-frying

1 Put the honey and lime in a small saucepan and heat gently, stirring. Turn off the heat but leave on the hob.

2 Sift the flours, baking powder and salt into a bowl.

3 Whisk in the soda water.

4 Trim the stalk from the flower heads to just where it branches into the flowers.

5 Heat the oil until a cube of day-old bread browns in 30 seconds.

6 Dip the heads in the batter and allow excess to drain off. Fry, turning over if necessary, until crisp and golden. Drain on kitchen paper.

7 Serve on small plates with the lime honey drizzled over.

Cool, sharp and refreshing, this sorbet makes the most of kiwis whilst they are at their best and most flavoursome. It's packed with vitamin C, too. I like to serve it in brandy snap baskets, which you can buy if you don't want to bother to make them yourself. Alternatively, just hand some wafers or shortbread separately.

Refreshing kiwi fruit and lime sorbet

1 Thinly pare the zest from the limes. Put the zest with the sugar and water in a heavy-based saucepan. Heat gently, stirring, until the sugar dissolves. Bring to the boil and boil for about 5 minutes until syrupy but don't allow to caramelise. Leave to cool.

2 Squeeze the juice and put in a blender. Peel two of the kiwi fruit and add to the blender. Run the machine to purée the fruit. Alternatively, rub the fruit through a sieve and mix with the juice. Tip into a freezerproof container.

3 Strain the cool syrup into the lime juice and kiwi fruit. Mix well.

4 Freeze for about 2 hours until firm around the edges. Tip into a bowl and whisk with a fork to break up the ice crystals.

5 Whisk the egg whites until stiff and fold into the mixture with a metal spoon. Tip back into the freezerproof container and freeze until firm. Transfer to the fridge about 20 minutes before eating to soften slightly.

6 Peel the remaining kiwi fruit and slice. Serve the sorbet in scoops in glass dishes with a slice of kiwi to decorate each dish.

Serves 4

2 limes
100 g granulated sugar
250 ml water
3 ripe kiwi fruit
2 egg whites

Summer is finally here! As the month progresses there should be an abundance of fresh fruit and vegetables for you to enjoy. **Strawberries** are at their peak, **cherries** and **gooseberries** are superb, too. The first **redcurrants** should be available and you may find **blackcurrants** coming in towards the end of the month but they are better in a few weeks' time. **Runner beans** and **broad beans, peas, sorrel** and **lettuces** are all superb. **Fennel** is in season but not at its peak, along with **globe artichokes, mangetout** and **cucumbers.** They are still worth buying but, remember, they will get even better! **Spring lamb** is now at its best to enjoy roasted, grilled, fried or barbecued, if the weather is kind.

June

Vegetables

Asparagus, aubergines, *broad beans*, broccoli, *carrots, cauliflowers*, courgettes, cucumbers, Florence fennel, globe artichokes, green garlic, *lettuces*, mangetout, new potatoes, *peas*, pea shoots, *radishes*, *rhubarb (outdoor)*, *rocket, runner beans*, *sorrel*, spring onions, turnips, *watercress*

Fruit and nuts

Avocados (Fuerte, Hass), *cherries*, *elderflowers, gooseberries*, kiwi fruit, lychees, mangoes, redcurrants, *strawberries*, tomatoes

Meat, poultry and game

Lamb, quail, venison, *wood pigeon*

Fish and seafood

Bream, brown shrimps, cod, *crabs, crayfish*, Dover sole, Dublin Bay prawns (scampi), haddock, halibut, herring, John Dory, lemon sole, lobster, *mackerel*, plaice, *pollack*, prawns, river trout (brown, rainbow), salmon, sardines, *sea bass, sea trout*

Foods in season

Foods in *italics* are foods from the UK at the peak of their season.

June

If you can't find sorrel, you can make this with extra lettuce. In fact, you can make a lovely simple lettuce soup without either the sorrel or asparagus! However, the combination of all three makes a delicate, light soup that's equally delicious served hot or chilled.

Sorrel, lettuce and asparagus summer soup

Serves 4

25 g butter
1 onion, finely chopped
1 large potato, diced
1 round lettuce, shredded
50 g sorrel, shredded
100 g asparagus, stalks trimmed
  and chopped
1 litre chicken or vegetable stock,
  ideally fresh or made with
  2 stock cubes
1 tsp chopped fresh thyme
Salt and freshly ground black
  pepper
A good pinch of grated nutmeg
6 tbsp single cream

1 Melt the butter in a saucepan. Add the onion and fry for 2 minutes, stirring, until softened but not browned.

2 Add the potato, lettuce, sorrel, asparagus, stock, thyme and a little salt and pepper. Bring to the boil, reduce the heat, part-cover and simmer for 20 minutes until the potato is really tender.

3 Purée the mixture in a blender or food processor. Rub through a sieve back into the pan and stir in the nutmeg and cream.

4 To serve hot, reheat gently without allowing the soup to boil. To serve cold, cool, then chill.

This is like a new version of Melanzana Parmigiana, which is slices of cooked aubergine with tomatoes and Mozzarella. I love the clean taste of soft goats' cheese, which has more flavour than Mascarpone, for instance. You could make your pesto from scratch but a good-quality jar works just fine.

Griddled aubergine with tomato, pesto and goats' cheese

Serves 4

2 aubergines, each sliced in four lengthways
Olive oil
4 tsp tomato purée
125 g soft goats' cheese
4 tsp fresh torn basil
Freshly ground black pepper
For the pesto dressing:
1½ tbsp pesto from a jar
2 tsp white balsamic condiment

1 Brush the aubergine slices on both sides with olive oil. Cook in an electric griddle for about 4 minutes or in a preheated griddle pan for about 4 minutes on each side, pressing down well with a spatula, until cooked and lined.

2 Spread the cut side of the four outer slices (purple on one side) with the tomato purée. Place on four small serving plates. Top with the goats' cheese, torn basil and some black pepper (you'll get a lovely marbled effect with the tomato and cheese).

3 Lay the other slices of aubergine across the cheese at an angle so you can still see the cheese, tomato and basil.

4 Whisk the pesto with 2 tbsp of olive oil and the balsamic condiment.

5 Trickle around the aubergines and serve while still warm.

This has a Middle Eastern flavour from the combination of tahini (sesame seed paste), chick peas, cumin, coriander and olives. It works with any white or oily fish fillets, so it's very versatile. You need a cooling salad to accompany it and you could try cucumber in minted yoghurt dressing instead of tomato and Feta.

Bream with tahini on crushed chick peas with olives

Serves 4

3 tbsp olive oil
1 onion, finely chopped
½ tsp ground cumin
425 g can of chick peas, drained
50 g sliced black olives
4 black bream, filleted
2 tbsp tahini paste
Finely grated zest and juice of
    1 lime
1 garlic clove, crushed
2 tbsp Greek-style yoghurt
2 tbsp milk
1 tbsp chopped fresh coriander
1 tbsp chopped fresh parsley
Salt and freshly ground black
    pepper
Sprigs of coriander or parsley, for
    garnishing
To serve:
Tomato and Feta cheese salad

1 Heat 2 tbsp of the oil in a saucepan. Add the onion and fry, stirring, for 4 minutes until lightly golden. Add the cumin and cook for 30 seconds. Stir in the drained chick peas and crush with the back of a wooden spoon against the side of the pan. They should still have a lot of texture.

2 Add the olives and remove from the heat.

3 Heat the remaining oil in a frying pan. Add the bream, skin-sides up, and brown for 2 minutes. Turn over.

4 Mix the remaining ingredients together with salt and pepper to taste. Spoon over the fish. Cook for 1 minute. Place the pan under a moderate grill and grill for a further 3 minutes until bubbling and turning lightly golden.

6 Meanwhile, reheat the chick peas.

7 Spoon the chick peas on to four warm plates. Top with the fish and sauce and garnish with sprigs of fresh coriander or parsley.

8 Serve with a tomato and Feta cheese salad.

These are gorgeous cooked on a barbecue but I suggest you use a hinged wire rack to cook them as they are tricky to turn when cooked over the coals. Make sure they are very fresh, with bright eyes and shiny not slimy skin. Ask the fishmonger to prepare them for you.

Fresh grilled sardines with lime, herbs and sea salt

1 Lay the fish on a sheet of foil on the grill rack.

2 Whisk the remaining ingredients except the salt together. Pour a little into a separate container and brush all over the fish.

3 Grill for about 3–4 minutes on each side, brushing frequently with the herb mixture until golden and cooked through.

4 Transfer to warm plates and trickle the remaining dressing over. Sprinkle with the sea salt and serve with lots of crusty bread.

Serves 4

12–16 fresh sardines, cleaned, and boned (if liked), leaving on the heads and tails
Finely grated zest and juice of 1 lime
150 ml olive oil
1 tbsp chopped fresh parsley
1 tbsp chopped fresh thyme
2 tsp chopped fresh tarragon
2 tsp snipped fresh chives
Freshly ground black pepper
2 tsp coarse sea salt
To serve:
Crusty bread

This is a lovely fresh combination of the tenderest lamb cutlets quickly grilled and glazed in honey then served on a bed of new potatoes, peas and cucumber in a light minted cream, mildly laced with dry vermouth. It needs nothing more to make a perfect summer lunch or dinner dish.

Honey-glazed spring lamb cutlets with minted peas and potatoes

Serves 4

450 g baby new potatoes, scraped
450 g fresh peas, shelled
Salt and freshly ground black
    pepper
8–12 lamb cutlets
2 tbsp sunflower oil
25 g unsalted butter
1 small onion, finely chopped
½ cucumber, skinned, seeded and
    diced
2 tbsp dry vermouth
120 ml crème fraîche
2 tbsp chopped fresh mint
2 tbsp clear honey
Small sprigs of mint, for garnishing

1 Cook the potatoes in boiling, lightly salted water for about 10 minutes until just tender. Drain.

2 Cook the peas in a separate pan for about 5 minutes until just tender. Drain.

3 Meanwhile, scrape the bones of the cutlets with a sharp knife, to leave them clean with the eye of meat intact. Lay them on foil on the grill rack and brush with the oil on both sides. If there is lots of meat on the bones, cut it off in a piece and cook alongside; it can be laid underneath for presentation.

4 Melt the butter in the rinsed-out potato saucepan. Add the onion and fry, stirring, for 2 minutes. Add the cucumber and cook, stirring, for a further 2 minutes.

5 Add the potatoes, peas, the vermouth, crème fraîche and mint. Cook, stirring gently, until bubbling. Season to taste. Keep warm.

6 Grill the cutlets for 1½ minutes on each side to brown. Brush with the honey and grill for a further 1 minute on each side until glazed and golden but still pink in the middle.

7 Spoon the pea and potato mixture on to warm plates. Lay the cutlets up against the mixture, bones pointing upwards. Garnish with small sprigs of mint and serve hot.

Quail are farmed all year round as they are a protected species in the wild but they are always considered to be at their best in the summer. If you have large appetites, serve two birds each and double the rub ingredients. The salsa incorporates the best British-grown ingredients with lovely fresh mango. Serve with rice or couscous.

Spatchcocked quail with cajun rub and fresh mango salsa

1 Cut the quail either side of the backbone. Remove the backbone and open the birds out flat.

2 Mix the garlic with the onion, paprika, chilli powder, thyme, oregano, salt and honey. Smear and rub the mixture all over the quail. Wrap in foil and leave in the fridge to marinate for at least 3 hours.

3 With the skin still on the mango, cut the flesh off the stone in three or four pieces, following the contour of the stone with the knife. Score the flesh one way then the other to make small dice, then cut the flesh off the skin into a bowl.

4 Add the green pepper, onion, cucumber, tomatoes, and chilli.

5 Whisk 2 tbsp of the oil with the lime zest and juice and the sugar. Season to taste and stir into the salsa with the coriander. Chill until ready to serve.

6 Heat the remaining oil in a frying pan. Add the quail and brown for 2 minutes on each side. Add the stock, cover and cook gently for about 10 minutes until tender. Transfer the birds to warm plates.

7 Boil the juices rapidly to reduce slightly and spoon over the birds. Spoon the salsa to one side, garnish with small wedges of lime and serve with rice or couscous.

Serves 4

4 quail
1 garlic clove, crushed
1 small onion, grated
2 tbsp paprika
$\frac{1}{2}$ tsp chilli powder
$\frac{1}{2}$ tsp dried thyme
1 tsp dried oregano
$\frac{1}{2}$ tsp salt
1 tsp clear honey
120 ml chicken stock
Lime wedges, for garnishing
For the salsa:
1 mango
1 green pepper, chopped
1 small onion, finely chopped
5 cm piece of cucumber, chopped
2 tomatoes, chopped
1 green chilli, seeded and chopped
3 tbsp olive oil
Grated zest and juice of $\frac{1}{2}$ lime
1 tsp light brown sugar
Freshly ground black pepper
1 tbsp chopped fresh coriander

This is lovely as a starter, light lunch or a side dish with cold meats or fish. You can, of course, vary the selection of vegetables according to what you can get locally. The important thing is to cook them lightly, so they still have some texture before coating them in the light, lemony mayonnaise.

Baby vegetable salad in garlic ciabatta crusts

Serves 4

4 ciabatta rolls
75 g butter, softened
1 large garlic clove, crushed
8 baby carrots, halved
4 runner beans, cut in diagonal slices
225 g fresh peas, shelled
8 asparagus spears, cut in short lengths
2 tbsp mayonnaise
2 tsp olive oil
$\frac{1}{2}$ tsp lemon juice
A good pinch of caster sugar
Salt and freshly ground black pepper

1 Cut a slice off the top of each roll and pull out most of the soft bread inside (use for breadcrumbs).

2 Mash the butter with the garlic and spread all over the inside and outside of each roll and the 'lids'. Place on a baking sheet.

3 Bake in a preheated oven at 180°C/gas 4/fan oven 160°C for about 15 minutes until golden. Remove from the oven and leave to cool and crisp.

4 Meanwhile, cook the carrots in boiling, lightly salted water for 3 minutes. Add the remaining vegetables and cook for 4 minutes more until all the vegetables are almost tender but not soft. Drain, rinse with cold water and drain again.

5 Mix the mayonnaise with the olive oil, lemon juice and sugar and season to taste with salt and pepper. Reserve four asparagus spear heads for garnishing, then fold the remaining cooked vegetables into the mayonnaise.

6 Transfer the ciabatta crusts to small serving plates. Spoon in the vegetables and garnish each with a reserved asparagus spear head and lay the 'lids' on top at an angle.

This makes a fabulous light lunch with crusty bread or can be served with eggs, fish or chicken as a side dish. If you're vegetarian, simply omit the bacon or add some diced firm tofu instead. I like to cut the beans in chunky diamonds instead of the more usual diagonal thin slices but you can prepare them like that, if you prefer.

Sweet and sour runner beans with bacon

1 Boil the beans in lightly salted water for about 5 minutes until just tender. Drain.

2 Heat the oil in the rinsed-out pan and fry the onion, garlic, bacon and mushrooms for 3–4 minutes, stirring.

3 Add the beans and the remaining ingredients and toss over a gentle heat until hot. Serve straight away.

Serves 4–6

900 g runner beans, stringed and cut in 2.5 cm diagonal chunks
2 tbsp olive oil
1 onion, finely chopped
1 garlic clove, crushed
6 rashers streaky bacon, diced
100 g button mushrooms, sliced
2 tbsp Worcestershire sauce
1 tbsp soy sauce
2 tbsp clear honey
2 tbsp cider vinegar

I like to use round brioches for this dish but they seem to be getting more difficult to come by. If they are not available, use the long rolls instead, although they don't look quite so attractive. Use the pulled out breadcrumbs for chocolate truffles with half the chocolate fondant recipe on page 26 and a dash of rum essence, then roll in cocoa.

Strawberry brioche summer puddings

Serves 4

4 brioches
350 g strawberries, hulled and
    sliced or left whole if small
50 g caster sugar
4 tbsp water
2 tsp lemon juice
To serve:
Crème fraîche

1 Cut a slice off the tops of the brioches and pull out most of the bread, leaving a shell about 7 mm wide.

2 Put the strawberries in a pan with the remaining ingredients. Bring to the boil, reduce the heat to moderate and cook for about 5 minutes until the sugar melts and the juices run but the fruit still has some shape. Leave to cool.

3 Brush all round the sides of each brioche with some of the juice then put on small plates. Pack the fruit and juice into the shells.

4 Chill overnight to allow the juices to soak through the buns. Serve with crème fraîche.

Sweet fresh cherries, mingled with a splash of kirsch in a sweet creamy ice, is a lovely way to finish a summer meal. The same principle can be used with raspberries and framboise liqueur, strawberries and fraise liqueur (or use brandy) or blackcurrants and cassis. You may need to add extra sugar for blackcurrants.

Fresh cherry and kirsch ice-cream

1 Put the chopped cherries in a saucepan with half the sugar and the lemon juice. Heat gently, stirring, until the sugar melts and the juices run. Leave to cool.

2 Whisk the egg whites until stiff then, in a separate bowl, whisk the egg yolks with the remaining sugar until thick and pale.

3 Whip the cream with the kirsch until softly peaking.

4 Fold the fruit into the egg yolk mixture then fold in the cream and, finally, the egg whites. Pack into a freezerproof container.

5 Cover and freeze for several hours or overnight until firm.

Serves 4

450 g fresh cherries, stoned and
    roughly chopped
100 g caster sugar
2 tsp lemon juice
4 eggs, separated
300 ml double cream
3 tbsp kirsch

This is the time of year to indulge in such delights as a **lobster** or **crab** salad (just your favourite salad ingredients with the fresh cooked seafood and some mayonnaise). You have a wide choice of glorious vegetables and fruits – from **courgettes** and **cauliflowers** to **gooseberries**, **raspberries** and **tomatoes**. You might even be lucky enough to take a stroll over the hills to pick tiny blue **bilberries** or **whortleberries**. Even with the glut of home-grown produce it's still worth checking that you're buying British because we're still importing mountains of the foods we also grow here – how mad is that? Look out for all the sweet juicy **soft fruits**, at their peak now, but it's also a good time for imported fruits like **peaches** and **nectarines**. English **veal** is excellent now. It's not reared in crates, as in some other countries, so is not such a pale colour. It's simply very young, tender, male beef. Try it.

July

Vegetables

Aubergines, *beetroot*, broad beans, broccoli, *carrots*, *cauliflowers*, *courgettes*, *cucumbers*, *Florence fennel*, *garlic*, *globe artichokes*, *green beans*, green garlic, *herbs*, *kohlrabi*, *lettuces*, *mangetout*, *new potatoes*, *onions*, *peas*, peppers, *potatoes (old, maincrop)*, *radishes*, *rocket*, runner beans, *samphire*, *sorrel*, sweetcorn, *Swiss chard*, turnips, *watercress*

Fruit and nuts

Apricots, avocados (Fuerte, Hass), *bilberries/whortleberries*, blackberries, *blackcurrants*, *blueberries*, *gooseberries*, greengages, kiwi fruit, loganberries, lychees, mangoes, melons, nectarines, peaches, *raspberries*, *redcurrants*, *strawberries*, *tomatoes*, *white currants*

Meat, poultry and game

Lamb, quail, *rabbit, veal (English)*, venison, *wood pigeon*

Fish and seafood

Bream, brown shrimps, cod, *crabs, crayfish*, Dover sole, *Dublin Bay prawns (scampi)*, haddock, herring, John Dory, lemon sole, *lobster, mackerel*, plaice, *pollack, prawns*, river trout (brown, rainbow), salmon, sardines, *scallops, sea bass, sea trout*

Foods in season

Foods in *italics* are foods from the UK at the peak of their season.

Artichokes can be served hot with melted butter or cold with plain French dressing. Alternatively, the small leaves and hairy chokes can be removed after cooking and the centres filled with a savoury stuffing. I like this more exciting dip for a change. Have a bowl on the table for the discarded sucked leaves and the hairy chokes.

Artichokes with black olive and oregano dressing

Serves 4

4 globe artichokes
1 tbsp lemon juice
For the dressing:
6 tbsp olive oil
3 tbsp red wine vinegar
25 g stoned black olives, chopped
1 tbsp chopped fresh oregano
2 tsp clear honey
½ tsp Dijon mustard
Salt and freshly ground black
  pepper

1 Hold the flower heads firmly and twist off the stalks (the strings will come away in the stalks).

2 Trim the points off the leaves, if liked. Cook in boiling, lightly salted water, to which the lemon juice has been added, for about 25 minutes or until a leaf pulls away easily from the head. Drain, rinse with cold water and drain again. Leave to cool.

3 Meanwhile, make the dressing. Whisk the ingredients together with salt and pepper to taste. Spoon into small serving dishes.

4 Place the artichokes on serving plates with the little dishes of dressing to one side.

5 To eat: pull off each leaf, dip in the dressing then pull the base through your teeth to suck off the fleshy part. Repeat until all the large leaves are eaten. Pull off the central, tiny, non-fleshy leaves then cut off the hairy choke. Trickle the remaining dressing over the heart and eat with a knife and fork.

July

This variation on a classic uses green garlic with its sweet delicate flavour when roasted, juicy ripe home-grown tomatoes and fresh basil on fried ciabatta. It makes a snack or appetiser to relish. You could add olives, anchovies or Mozzarella, too, but really, the simple, perfect flavours are unbeatable.

Bruschetta with roasted green garlic, tomatoes and fresh basil

1 Heat half the oil in a frying pan. Add the garlic and fry for about 2 minutes over a gentle heat, shaking the pan, until the garlic is lightly golden. Do not allow to burn or it will be bitter.

2 Lift the garlic out of the pan on to a small plate and mash thoroughly with a knife.

3 Add the remaining oil to the pan and fry the ciabatta slices on both sides until golden.

4 Spread the slices with the mashed garlic. Mix the tomatoes with the chopped basil and some black pepper and spoon on top of the fried ciabatta.

5 Sprinkle each slice with just a few grains of coarse sea salt.

Serves 4

4 tbsp olive oil
4 green garlic cloves, peeled but left whole
8 slices of ciabatta bread
4 ripe tomatoes, skinned and chopped
1 tbsp chopped fresh basil
Freshly ground black pepper
A few grains of coarse sea salt

I first created this with fresh tuna – but that's not seasonal or British! Mackerel is an underrated, superb fish with a wonderful flavour, very inexpensive and full of goodness. Cooking it in this way with pickled pink ginger, fresh stir-fried vegetables, soy sauce and rice makes an impressive, colourful meal.

Stuffed mackerel with pickled ginger on oriental vegetables

Serves 4

4 mackerel, cleaned, heads
   removed, if liked
25 g pickled sliced sushi ginger
3 tbsp soy sauce
2 tbsp sunflower oil
1 garlic clove, crushed
1 red pepper, thinly sliced
1 green pepper, thinly sliced
1 bunch of spring onions, cut in
   short lengths
2 carrots, cut in matchsticks
1/4 cucumber, cut in matchsticks
100 g mangetout
225 g fresh egg noodles
A good pinch of Chinese five-spice
   powder

1 Rinse the fish inside and out and pat dry on kitchen paper. Make several slashes on both sides of the fish with a sharp knife.

2 Pack half the ginger inside the fish and rub the outsides with 1 tbsp of the soy sauce and 1 tbsp of the oil.

3 Place on foil on a grill rack and grill for 5 minutes on each side until crisp, golden brown and cooked through.

4 Meanwhile, heat the remaining oil in a wok or large frying pan. Add the prepared vegetables and stir-fry for 3 minutes. Add the remaining ginger and noodles and toss for 1 minute.

5 Add the remaining soy and the five-spice powder and toss to coat.

6 Pile the oriental vegetables and noodles on to warm plates. Top each with a mackerel and serve hot.

This is an exciting change from the more normal tuna or anchovy-based salad. It has all the lovely fresh summer vegetables, blended with a light dressing and succulent, fresh prawns. You can, of course, substitute the other fish instead. Alternatively, try it with some cooked, flaked salmon or, if you can get them, freshwater crayfish.

Prawn Niçoise
with summer vegetables

1 Cook the potatoes in boiling, lightly salted water for about 8 minutes until tender. Add the beans after 4 minutes and add the asparagus for the last 2 minutes. Drain, rinse with cold water and drain again.

2 Tip into a bowl and add the onion, tomatoes, cucumber, lettuce, rocket, prawns and olives.

3 Whisk the remaining ingredients, except the eggs, together and pour over the salad. Toss gently then pile into serving bowls or on large serving plates.

4 Shell the eggs and cut in quarters. Arrange on top of the salads.

Serves 4

350 g new potatoes, scraped and cut in bite-sized pieces
100 g French beans, topped, tailed and cut in short lengths
100 g asparagus, cut in short lengths
1 small red onion, thinly sliced
4 tomatoes, quartered
1/4 cucumber, cut in small chunks
1 Little Gem lettuce, torn in pieces
1 handful of rocket
400 g fresh cooked peeled prawns
12 black olives
1 tsp chopped fresh oregano
4 tbsp olive oil
1 tbsp white wine vinegar
Salt and freshly ground black pepper
1/2 tsp Dijon mustard
1/2 tsp anchovy essence
1/2 tsp caster sugar
Salt and freshly ground black pepper
4 hard-boiled eggs

The salami adds an exciting Mediterranean flavour to the golden, crumb-coated escalopes and the cheese adds gooey moistness. You could use ham instead of salami and ring the changes with other melting cheeses, like Cheddar, Monterey Jack or a Swiss cheese, like Emmental.

Veal escalope sandwiches with salami and Gouda

Serves 4

4 veal escalopes, halved
12 slices of salami
4–8 slices of Gouda (enough to top 4 slices of the meat)
8 fresh basil leaves
Salt and freshly ground black pepper
1 egg, beaten
100 g fresh breadcrumbs
4 tbsp olive oil
Lemon wedges and 4 small sprigs of basil, for garnishing
To serve:
Sautéed potatoes and Glazed Vine-ripened Cherry Tomatoes in Sherry Vinegar (see page 75)

1 Sandwich the veal escalopes together in pairs with the salami, cheese and basil leaves. Season lightly.

2 Dip in beaten egg then breadcrumbs to coat completely. Chill, if time, until ready to cook.

3 Heat the oil in a frying pan and fry the escalopes over a moderate heat for about 3–4 minutes on each side until golden brown and cooked through.

4 Drain on kitchen paper. Transfer to warm plates, garnish with lemon wedges and sprigs of basil and serve with sautéed potatoes and the glazed tomatoes.

Photograph opposite:
Vegetable couscous with spices and fresh coriander (see page 147)

In a restaurant you would have a small half shoulder to yourself. I think this is too much so I've chopped a shoulder in four. By all means cook four half shoulders if you prefer, just double the quantity of flavourings. Ask your butcher to chop the lamb for you.

Slow-roast lamb with rosemary, Pimms and fresh redcurrants

1 Make tiny slits in the lamb flesh all over with the sharp point of a knife.

2 Push a sliver of garlic into each hole. Lay a small sprig of rosemary on top of each lamb quarter. Place in a roaster-baster or roasting tin with the stock, Pimms and redcurrant jelly. Season with salt and freshly ground black pepper.

3 Cover the tin with the lid or foil and roast in a preheated oven at 160°C/gas 3/fan oven 145°C for 3 hours, until very tender.

4 Lift out the meat on to a warm plate. Remove all the dried-up sprigs of rosemary and discard. Keep the meat warm.

5 Select 4 small sprigs of redcurrants for garnishing. Remove the rest of the redcurrants from their stalks with the prongs of a fork.

6 Spoon off any excess fat from the juices in the meat tin. Bring to the boil, throw in the redcurrants and boil for 3–4 minutes until reduced and slightly thickened. Taste and re-season, if necessary.

7 Transfer the lamb to four warm serving plates. Spoon the redcurrant juices over. Push a small sprig of rosemary into each piece of meat and drape a sprig of redcurrants around the meat. Serve hot with new potatoes and mangetout.

Serves 4

1 shoulder of lamb, chopped in quarters
2 garlic cloves, cut in slivers
8 small sprigs of fresh rosemary
150 ml lamb or beef stock, ideally fresh or made with $\frac{1}{2}$ stock cube
3 tbsp Pimms No 1
2 tbsp redcurrant jelly
Salt and freshly ground black pepper
175 g fresh redcurrants
To serve:
New potatoes and mangetout

Photograph opposite:
Warm turkey strip salad with radicchio and cranberries
(see page 156)

Swiss chard is often served as two vegetables: the green part as greens and the stalks like asparagus with melted butter. Here the stalks are steamed with a drizzle of olive oil and the greens are shredded and sautéed with pine nuts and sun-dried tomatoes, then the two are arranged together as a colourful starter or accompaniment to grills.

Swiss chard in two halves with tomatoes and pine nuts

Serves 4

450 g Swiss chard
Salt
50 g pine nuts
4 tbsp olive oil
4 sun-dried tomatoes, chopped
Freshly ground black pepper
1 tbsp balsamic vinegar
25 g fresh Parmesan shavings

1 Trim off a thin sliver from the base of the Swiss chard stalks, then cut them off from the green tops. Place in a steamer, sprinkle very lightly with salt and steam for 5 minutes.

2 Roll up the chard leaves and shred. Heat a large frying pan. Add the pine nuts and fry, shaking the pan, until golden. Immediately tip out of the pan and reserve.

3 Heat half the oil in the pan and stir-fry the shredded greens for 2 minutes until wilted.

4 Add the pine nuts, sun-dried tomatoes and a little salt and pepper and toss for 1 minute. Add the balsamic vinegar and toss again.

5 Pile the greens in the centre of a warm serving dish and arrange the steamed stalks around the edge. Trickle the stalks with the remaining olive oil and scatter the Parmesan shavings over them.

Serve this rich but simple dish as a starter, side dish or light lunch (with crusty bread and a salad). If you want added depth – and don't mind the extra calories – fry the slices in a little olive oil and butter until golden instead of boiling them in water.

Three cheese courgette gratin with fresh sage

1 Cook the courgettes in boiling, lightly salted water for 3–4 minutes until just tender but still with some 'bite'. Drain thoroughly then dry on kitchen paper.

2 Tip the courgettes into an ovenproof serving dish.

3 Mix the crème fraîche with the sage, Cheddar, Red Leicester, 15 g of the Parmesan and the beaten eggs. Season to taste.

4 Spoon over the courgettes and sprinkle with the remaining Parmesan. Bake in a preheated oven at 190°C/gas 5/fan oven 170°C for about 35 minutes until bubbling and golden on top.

Serves 4

4–6 courgettes, depending on size, sliced
Salt
200 g crème fraîche
1 tsp chopped fresh sage
40 g Cheddar cheese, grated
40 g Red Leicester cheese, grated
40 g Parmesan cheese, freshly grated
2 eggs, beaten
Freshly ground black pepper

Gooseberries have a short season, so it's worth enjoying them while you can. Here they are gently cooked and puréed with some sugar then topped with creamy homemade custard and dusted with a little freshly grated nutmeg. If elderflowers are still around, add a handful when stewing the gooseberries.

Creamy gooseberry and custard layer

Serves 4

450 g gooseberries
100 g caster sugar
300 ml milk
2 tbsp cornflour
150 ml single cream
2 eggs, beaten
A few drops of vanilla essence
A little freshly grated nutmeg, to decorate

1 Put the gooseberries in a saucepan with 75 g of the sugar. Heat very gently, stirring, until the juices run, then cover and cook gently for 10 minutes until the fruit is pulpy, stirring occasionally.

2 Purée in a blender or food processor then rub through a sieve to remove the pips and stalks.

3 Blend the remaining sugar with 150 ml of the milk and the cornflour in a saucepan. Stir in the remaining milk and the cream. Bring to the boil and cook for 1 minute, stirring all the time. Remove from the heat.

4 Whisk a little of the sauce into the beaten eggs, then tip into the rest of the sauce. Return to a gentle heat and whisk all the time until thickened. Add vanilla essence to taste.

5 Spoon the gooseberry purée into glasses. Gently spoon the custard over. Dust with a little grated nutmeg, leave to cool, then chill until ready to serve.

This looks and tastes so pretty, it's a shame to cut it! A ring of pale, almost white, light-as-air cake, with a speckling of pale green pistachios, smothered with sweetened cream and quark – a light soft curd cheese – and filled with a mixture of blueberries and raspberries.

Blueberry, raspberry and pistachio angel cake

1 Put the pistachios in a bowl and cover with boiling water. Leave to stand for 5 minutes then drain and rub off the skins in a new disposable dishcloth. Finely chop half of the nuts.

2 Dust a 1 litre ring tin with flour.

3 Whisk the egg whites until foamy. Whisk in the salt and cream of tartar and whisk until stiff. Whisk in 1 tbsp of the sugar to keep the eggs stable.

4 Sift the flours with the remaining sugar. Sprinkle half over the egg whites and fold in with a metal spoon. Repeat with the rest of the flour mixture, the chopped pistachios and essences.

5 Turn into the prepared tin and level the surface. Bake in a preheated oven at 160°C/gas 3/fan oven 145°C for about 30 minutes until golden and firm to the touch. Leave to cool in the tin then turn out on to a plate or board.

6 Whip the cream and sifted icing sugar until peaking then whisk in the quark.

7 Spread the cream mixture all over the cake. Mix the blueberries and raspberries together and pile into the centre of the ring.

8 Scatter the remaining pistachios over the cake to decorate, then chill until ready to serve. Just before serving, dust a little sifted icing sugar over the fruit.

Serves 6–8

40 g shelled pistachio nuts
3 egg whites
A pinch of salt
$\frac{1}{2}$ tsp cream of tartar
100 g caster sugar
40 g plain flour, plus extra for dusting
20 g cornflour
A few drops of almond essence
A few drops of vanilla essence
For the filling and topping:
200 ml double cream
40 g icing sugar, plus extra for dusting
150 g quark
100 g blueberries
100 g raspberries

All the soft fruits are still around plus loads of colourful vegetables, including extra specialities like **sweetcorn** and **cavolo nero** – tall black cabbage that originated in Italy. You can enjoy fresh **chillies** and **peppers**, all the **salad** stuff and a glut of **fruit**. **Victoria plums** will begin to ripen and home-grown **melons** should be available along with the **soft fruits** and cultivated **blackberries**. **Squid** and **scallops** are really good and you could be lucky enough to find **whitebait**. The **grouse** season also starts on the 12th. If you can find **samphire**, do try it. Cook it in boiling, unsalted water for 2–5 minutes until the flesh pulls easily off the stalks. Drizzle it with melted butter and draw it through the teeth to pull off the flesh. Alternatively, cut it in short lengths and add it to a Niçoise salad or a seafood pasta or risotto.

August

Vegetables

Aubergines, beetroot, broad beans, *broccoli,* cavolo nero, *carrots, chillies, courgettes, cucumbers, Florence fennel, garlic, globe artichokes, green beans, kohlrabi, lettuces, mangetout, onions, peas, peppers, potatoes (old, maincrop),* radishes, *rocket, runner beans, samphire, sorrel, sweetcorn, Swiss chard, watercress*

Fruit and nuts

Apricots, avocados (Hass), *blackberries, blackcurrants, blueberries,* greengages, *loganberries,* mangoes, *melons,* nectarines, pawpaws, peaches, *plums, raspberries, redcurrants, tayberries, tomatoes, white currants*

Meat, poultry and game

Grouse, lamb, quail, *rabbit,* venison, *wood pigeon*

Fish and seafood

Bream, brown shrimps, cod, *crabs, crayfish,* Dover sole, Dublin Bay prawns (scampi), grey mullet, haddock, halibut, herring, John Dory, lemon sole, *lobster, mackerel,* monkfish, plaice, *pollack,* red mullet, *river trout (brown, rainbow),* salmon, sardines, *scallops, sea bass, squid, whitebait*

Foods in season

Foods in *italics* are foods from the UK at the peak of their season.

This is a variation on a traditional theme but it's too good not to include in this book. It's fresh, clean-tasting and cooling on a hot summer's day. You can add prawns or crab to it, or even some diced ham but I prefer it just plain and simple. It's particularly good with slices of rye bread spread with unsalted butter.

Chilled cucumber and fresh dill soup

Serves 4

1 cucumber
Salt and freshly ground black pepper
2 tbsp chopped fresh dill
2 tbsp white balsamic condiment
284 ml buttermilk
300 ml milk
4 tiny sprigs of dill, for garnishing

1 Cut four thin slices off the cucumber and reserve for garnish. Grate the remainder into a large bowl. Sprinkle with salt, toss and leave to stand for 30 minutes.

2 Squeeze out all the excess moisture and drain off.

3 Stir in the dill, balsamic condiment, buttermilk and pepper to taste. Cover, then chill for at least 1 hour to allow the flavours to develop.

4 Just before serving, stir in the milk, ladle into bowls and garnish each bowl with a slice of cucumber and a tiny sprig of dill. Serve cold.

Whitebait is delicious just tossed in seasoned flour, quickly fried and served with wedges of lemon. However, it's extra-special if you make a gremolata – chopped eggs with lime, olive oil, garlic and parsley to dip the crispy little morsels into. For added piquancy, you could add a teaspoon of chopped pickled capers to the mix.

Whitebait with lime and egg gremolata

1 Whisk the gremolata ingredients together, then chill.

2 Pick over the whitebait and discard any that are damaged.

3 Mix the flour with a little salt and pepper and use to coat the fish.

4 Heat the oil for deep-frying until a cube of day-old bread browns in 30 seconds. Deep-fry the whitebait in batches for 3 minutes until golden. Drain on kitchen paper and keep warm while cooking the remainder.

5 Spoon the gremolata into little individual pots. Pile the whitebait on to warm plates with a pot of gremolata on each plate. Serve straight away.

Serves 4

For the gremolata:
2 hard-boiled eggs, finely chopped
Finely grated zest and juice of 1 lime
A pinch of caster sugar
4 tbsp olive oil
2 garlic cloves, crushed
2 tbsp chopped fresh parsley
For the fish:
700 g whitebait
4 tbsp plain flour
Salt and freshly ground black pepper
Oil for deep-frying

Red harissa paste (or powder) is a mixture of chilli and loads of other spices and comes from North Africa. It has become very popular in this country over the past few years. It's hot but not searing and has a wonderful rich flavour that enhances fish, meat or poultry. You simply smear it on before frying or grilling.

Rainbow trout with harissa, green beans and tomatoes

Serves 4

4 rainbow trout, cleaned and heads removed, if liked
Salt and freshly ground black pepper
2 tbsp harissa paste
225 g fine green beans, trimmed
25 g unsalted butter
2 tbsp olive oil
12 cherry tomatoes, halved
A pinch of caster sugar
To serve:
New potatoes

1 Rinse the fish inside and out and pat dry with kitchen paper.

2 Make several slashes in both sides of the fish. Season with a little salt and pepper and rub the paste all over the skin and into the slits.

3 Cook the beans in boiling, lightly salted water for about 4 minutes until just tender but still bright green. Drain.

4 Meanwhile, melt half the butter with the oil in a large frying pan. Add the trout and fry for 5 minutes on each side until golden and cooked through.

5 Add the tomatoes, sugar, the remaining butter and a little salt and pepper to the bean pan and toss over a gentle heat for 2–3 minutes until the tomatoes are softening but still hold their shape. Return the beans to the pan and toss gently to heat through.

6 Pile the beans and tomatoes on to warm plates and put a trout on top of each pile. Serve with new potatoes.

It's important that the fish is extremely fresh for this dish. The cubes of salmon are 'cooked' by marinating them in fresh lime and tequila, mixed with fresh chilli, sweet peppers, avocado, onion and coriander for a delicious, very Mexican experience. It's wonderful made with monkfish, too.

Salmon ceviche with tequila, chilli and fresh lime

1 Cut the fish into bite-sized pieces. Place in a shallow dish and toss in the lime juice, tequila and chilli. Cover and leave to marinate in the fridge for at least 4 hours.

2 Mix the remaining ingredients together, then chill.

3 Spoon the pepper mixture on to four serving plates. Top with the fish. Garnish with lime wedges and serve with rolled up flour tortillas.

Serves 4

450 g very fresh salmon fillet, skinned
Juice of 2 limes
2 tbsp tequila
1 red chilli, seeded and finely chopped
1 green pepper, diced
1 red pepper, diced
1 avocado, peeled, halved, stoned and diced
1 small onion, finely chopped
2 tbsp chopped fresh coriander
2 tbsp olive oil
Salt and freshly ground black pepper
Lime wedges, for garnishing
To serve:
Flour tortillas, rolled up

You could serve this as a starter for eight or as a main course with some fresh egg or rice noodles or egg-fried rice. It looks sensational and is very easy to prepare. Nori sheets, usually used for sushi, are available in all good supermarkets and need no preparation. You simply roll the cooked chicken in a strip before cutting in slices.

Sesame chicken and nori wraps with chilli and ginger sauce

Serves 4 or 8

For the sauce:
1 green chilli, seeded and finely chopped
1 tsp grated fresh root ginger
2 garlic cloves, crushed
4 tbsp soy sauce, plus a few drops for the wraps
3 tbsp mirin (Japanese rice wine)
4 skinless chicken breasts
4 tsp sesame seeds
1 tsp sesame oil
1 tbsp sunflower oil
1 small carrot, cut in matchsticks
1 small red pepper, cut in matchsticks
1 small courgette, cut in matchsticks
2 spring onions, cut in short lengths and shredded
450 ml chicken stock, ideally fresh or made with 1 stock cube
4 nori sheets, halved

1 Mix the chilli with the ginger, one of the cloves of garlic, the soy sauce and rice wine in a small bowl. Leave to stand so the flavours develop.

2 Place the chicken breasts one at a time in a plastic bag and beat with a rolling pin or meat mallet until flattened. Sprinkle each with a few sesame seeds.

3 Heat the sesame and sunflower oils together in a wok or frying pan. Add the prepared vegetables and remaining garlic and stir-fry for 2 minutes. Turn down the heat, cover and cook for a further 3 minutes. Add a few drops of soy sauce and toss. Remove from the heat.

4 Divide the vegetables among the chicken then roll the pieces of chicken up. Return to the wok or frying pan.

5 Add the chicken stock. Bring to the boil, reduce the heat, cover and simmer very gently for about 10 minutes, turning once until tender and cooked through.

6 Lift out of the stock and drain. Roll each piece of chicken in a nori sheet, dampening the edges so they stick together. Cut the rolls in slices and arrange on white plates. Spoon a little of the cooking juices over the slices. Serve with the dipping sauce.

Large free-range pork chops are a delight to eat. The secret is to cook them quickly to brown them, then turn down the heat and cook until the meat feels just firm to the touch. If you continue to cook, they'll go hard and dry. Here they are flavoured with sage and topped with a colourful, sweet-spiced combination of aubergine, tomatoes and onion.

Pork chops with aubergine coulis

1 Heat the oil in a large frying pan. Add the aubergine, onion and garlic and fry, stirring, for about 6 minutes until soft.

2 Add the tomatoes, spices, sugar, lemon juice and a little salt and pepper and cook, stirring and turning, for a further 2 minutes until the mixture is thick but you can still identify the pieces of vegetables. Taste and re-season, if necessary. Tip into a small bowl. Keep warm.

3 Rinse out the pan. Melt the butter and add the chops. Fry quickly on both sides to brown. Season the chops, sprinkle with the sage, turn down the heat and fry for 5–8 minutes, turning once, until the flesh feels firm but is still juicy. They should be cooked through but not overdone.

4 Transfer the chops to warm plates. Add the stock to the pan and boil rapidly, scraping up any sediment until reduced. Season to taste. Spoon over the chops, put a spoonful of the coulis on top and serve with sautéed potatoes and green beans.

Serves 4

6 tbsp olive oil
1 aubergine, finely diced
1 onion, finely chopped
1 large garlic clove, crushed
2 tomatoes, finely chopped
$\frac{1}{2}$ tsp grated fresh root ginger
$\frac{1}{4}$ tsp ground cinnamon
$\frac{1}{2}$ tsp ground cumin
1 tsp light brown sugar
1 tsp lemon juice
Salt and freshly ground black pepper
15 g butter
4 large pork chops
1 tsp chopped fresh sage
150 ml pork or chicken stock, ideally fresh or made with $\frac{1}{2}$ stock cube
4 small sprigs of sage, for garnishing
To serve:
Sautéed potatoes and green beans

This lovely, colourful combination will delight veggies and meat eaters alike. It's a complete meal but you could serve it with some plain or fried rice. For a more substantial meal, have it as an accompaniment to Chinese ribs, grilled fish steaks, pork or chicken (brushed with soy sauce first).

Vegetable stir-fry with black beans

Serves 4

2 tbsp sunflower oil
1 garlic clove, crushed
1 onion, sliced
1 green pepper, diced
1 red pepper, diced
1 carrot, cut in matchsticks
1 courgette, sliced
175 g head of broccoli, cut in tiny
   florets
100 g mangetout
2 x 425 g cans of black beans,
   drained
2 tbsp black bean sauce
1 tbsp soy sauce
1 tbsp dry sherry

1 Heat the oil in a wok or large frying pan. Add the garlic, onion, peppers and carrot and stir-fry for 2 minutes.

2 Add the remaining vegetables and stir-fry for a further 3 minutes or until cooked to your liking.

3 Add the beans, sauces and sherry and toss for 2 minutes until piping hot.

These are gorgeous with any barbecued, grilled or roasted meats, chicken or fish. You can ring the changes by adding aubergines or courgettes to the mixture but always make sure you include some peppers for their distinctive Mediterranean flavour. You can chill them and serve cold as a salad if you prefer.

Roasted rainbow peppers with onions, rosemary and garlic

1 Spread out the peppers and onions in a large roasting tin. Scatter the garlic over.

2 Strip the leaves off the rosemary stalks and finely chop. Scatter over the peppers.

3 Trickle the olive oil all over and add a good grinding of pepper.

4 Roast in a preheated oven at 200°C/gas 6/fan oven 180°C for about 45 minutes until soft and lightly browned in places, stirring twice during cooking.

5 Tip with all the delicious flavoured oil into a serving dish and sprinkle with a few grains of coarse sea salt.

Serves 4

2 red peppers, cut in 6 pieces
2 green peppers, cut in 6 pieces
2 yellow peppers, cut in 6 pieces
2 orange peppers, cut in 6 pieces
2 red onions, cut in wedges
2 garlic cloves, finely chopped
1 large sprig of fresh rosemary
5 tbsp olive oil
Freshly ground black pepper
Coarse sea salt

The lovely light sponge, flavoured with the zest of an orange and drizzled with a rich loganberry sauce, is topped with fresh fruit to make a delicious summertime dessert. It can be made in advance then just put together at the last minute. You can use raspberries or strawberries instead of the loganberries if you like.

Orange sponge with fresh loganberry sauce

Serves 6

For the sponge:
75 g self-raising flour
1 tsp baking powder
100 g caster sugar
75 g butter, softened
1 large egg
Finely grated zest of 1 orange
2 tbsp milk
For the sauce and topping:
Juice of 1 orange
350 g fresh loganberries
2 tbsp icing sugar
To serve:
Crème fraîche

1 Oil an 18 cm/7 in square, shallow baking tin and line the base with non-stick baking parchment.

2 Put the flour, baking powder, 75 g of the sugar, the butter, egg, orange zest and milk in a bowl and beat well with a wooden spoon. Alternatively, mix in a food processor but run the machine only until the mixture is blended; do not over-mix.

3 Turn into the oiled tin and level the surface. Bake in a preheated oven at 190°C/gas 5/fan oven 170°C for about 25 minutes until risen, golden and the centre springs back when pressed gently. Cool slightly then turn out on to a wire rack to cool completely.

4 Put half the loganberries in a small saucepan with the orange juice and remaining caster sugar. Bring to the boil, reduce the heat and simmer for 5 minutes until pulpy.

5 Rub the stewed loganberries through a sieve to purée and remove the pips. Leave to cool.

6 When ready to serve, cut the cake into six pieces. Transfer to serving plates. Trickle the loganberry sauce over and around. Pile the remaining loganberries on top and decorate with a little sifted icing sugar. Put a spoonful of crème fraîche to the side of each plate and serve.

Peaches, nectarine, greengages or plums all taste fabulous given this treatment. Somehow the amaretto brings out the flavour of every single fruit in a slightly different way and the almond curls complement the fruit perfectly. I like the fruit served warm but you could chill them first if you prefer.

Poached apricots in amaretto with almond curls

1 Make the almond curls. Beat the butter with the sugar until light and fluffy. Work in the flour and almonds.

2 Line a baking sheet with non-stick baking parchment. Using a teaspoon, put the mixture in 12 small mounds, well apart, on the baking sheet. Flatten with a wet knife.

3 Bake in a preheated oven at 200°C/gas 6/fan oven 180°C for about 15 minutes until lightly golden. Lift off the baking sheet and quickly curl round a rolling pin. When firm, transfer to a wire rack.

4 Put the sugar and water in a saucepan and heat gently, stirring, until the sugar melts.

5 Add the fruit, bring to the boil, reduce the heat, cover and cook very gently for 5–10 minutes until the fruit is tender but still holds its shape. Do not boil rapidly or it will break up.

6 Add the amaretto, turn into a glass dish and leave until warm. Serve with the almond curls and pouring cream.

Serves 4

For the almond curls:
50 g butter, softened
50 g caster sugar
40 g plain flour
50 g flaked almonds
For the fruit:
50 g caster sugar
150 ml water
450 g fresh apricots, halved and stoned
2–3 tbsp amaretto liqueur
To serve:
Pouring cream

August

This month is a lovely mixture. You still have all the **summer fruit** and **vegetables** but the autumn is nearly upon us with **blackberries** and **elderberries** in the hedgerows, **figs**, **apples**, **damsons** and **hazelnuts** on the trees and **grouse**, **quail**, **guinea fowl**, **wild duck** and **pigeons** all available. It's also the time for **wild mushrooms**. You can forage for your own, if you know what you're doing, but you'll also find them sold locally. I have to say that getting up early on a dewy September morning to look for field mushrooms is one of life's simple and delightful pleasures.

September

Vegetables

Aubergines, beetroot, broccoli, butternut squash, cardoons, *carrots,* celery, *chillies, courgettes, cucumbers, curly kale, Florence fennel, garlic, globe artichokes, kohlrabi,* leeks, lettuces, *mangetout, marrows, onions, peppers, potatoes (old, maincrop),* radishes, *rocket, sweetcorn, Swiss chard, watercress, wild mushrooms (blewits, ceps, chanterelles, field, horse, oyster, parasol, puffballs)*

Fruit and nuts

Apples (Discovery, Russets, Worcester), avocados (Hass), *blackberries,* chestnuts, clementines, cranberries, *damsons, elderberries, figs, grapes, greengages, hazelnuts,* mangoes, melons, nectarines, pawpaws, peaches, *pears (William), plums, tomatoes*

September

Meat, poultry and game

Duck, goose, grouse, guinea fowl, lamb, *quail, rabbit,* venison, *wild duck (mallard), wood pigeon*

Fish and seafood

Bream, brown shrimps, clams, cod, *crabs,* Dublin Bay prawns (scampi), grey mullet, haddock, halibut, John Dory, lemon sole, *lobster, mackerel,* monkfish, plaice, *river trout (brown, rainbow), scallops, sea bass,* skate, *squid, turbot*

Foods in season

Foods in *italics* are foods from the UK at the peak of their season.

You can make this with a bought dressed crab, if you prefer. Simply scoop the meat out of the shell, keeping the dark and white meat separate and continue as from step 2. The flavour won't be quite as good as if you'd used the whole crab shell, body and all, for the stock, but it will save lots of time.

Fresh crab bisque with brandy and croûtons

Serves 4–6

1 fresh cooked crab
25 g butter
1 celery stick, chopped
1 onion, chopped
1 litre fish stock, ideally fresh or made with 1 stock cube
2 slices of wholemeal bread
3 tbsp olive oil
3 tbsp plain flour
150 ml milk
140 ml carton single cream
2 tbsp brandy
Salt and freshly ground black pepper

1 Take all the dark and white meat out of the crab body and claws. Keep them separate.

2 Melt the butter in a large saucepan, add the celery and onion and cook gently, stirring, for 2 minutes. Add the dark meat, all the crab shell, legs and body and the stock. Bring to the boil, reduce the heat, part-cover and simmer gently for 45 minutes. Strain.

3 Meanwhile, make the croûtons. Cut the crusts off the bread and cut into small cubes. Heat the oil in a frying pan and fry the bread, stirring and turning, for 2–3 minutes until golden. Drain on kitchen paper.

4 Blend the flour with the milk in the rinsed-out stock saucepan. Blend in the strained stock. Bring to the boil and cook for 2 minutes, stirring.

5 Add the white crab meat, cream and brandy and season to taste. Re-heat, stirring, but do not boil.

6 Ladle into warm bowls and scatter the croûtons on top. Serve immediately.

I first had a coarse pâté with hazelnuts in France, when I was a child. I thought it was magnificent. The nuts took on a delicate crunch when cooked with the meat and imparted a delightful flavour as well. I've tried to emulate what I remember and I'm rather pleased with the result. It's good as a starter but better for lunch.

Coarse pork liver terrine with hazelnuts

1 Line a 1.5 litre terrine or large loaf tin with some of the bacon rashers, trimming to fit as necessary.

2 Using a food processor or mincer, process the onion, garlic, herbs, pork, bacon and liver but not too finely.

3 Mix in the spices, port, hazelnuts, salt and a good grinding of pepper. Turn into the prepared dish and level the surface.

4 Top with the remaining bacon. Cover with greaseproof paper then a lid or foil and stand the terrine in a roasting tin containing 2.5 cm of boiling water.

5 Cook in a preheated oven at 160°C/gas 3/fan oven 145°C for 1½ hours or until firm to the touch.

6 Remove from the tin and remove the cover. Top with some clean greaseproof paper and weight down with heavy weights or cans of food. Leave until cold, then chill.

7 If liked (particularly if using a loaf tin rather than a terrine), loosen the edges and turn out on to a serving dish. Serve sliced with crusty bread, mustard and a side salad.

Serves 6–12

12 rashers streaky bacon, rinded
1 onion, quartered
2 garlic cloves
A small handful of fresh parsley
8 fresh sage leaves (or ½ tsp dried)
450 g belly pork, skinned
100 g unsmoked bacon pieces, trimmed of any rind or gristle
350 g pigs' liver
¼ tsp grated nutmeg
A good pinch of ground cloves
4 tbsp port
50 g shelled hazelnuts
1½ tsp salt
Freshly ground black pepper
To serve:
Crusty bread, mustard and a side salad

King scallops are at their finest now. They have very delicate flesh that needs only a couple of minutes' cooking. Here I've sautéed them in olive oil flavoured with green chillies, with some fresh Florence fennel and the zest and juice of a lime. You need lots of bread to mop up the sensational juices.

Sizzling scallops with lime, fennel and fresh chilli oil

Serves 4

8 tbsp olive oil
1–2 fresh green chillies, seeded and finely chopped
1 head of fennel, thinly sliced, reserving the green fronds
1 bunch of spring onions, chopped
12 king scallops with their corals
Thinly pared zest and juice of 1 lime
Salt and freshly ground black pepper
Cayenne
A few chive stalks, for garnishing
To serve:
French bread

1 Put the oil in a frying pan, add the chillies and cook very gently for 2 minutes to impart the chilli flavour into the oil as it heats.

2 Add the fennel and onion and fry gently for 3–4 minutes until soft but not brown. Lift out of the pan with a draining spoon and reserve.

3 Turn up the heat and add the scallops. Fry for 1 minute on each side until lightly golden and just cooked but still soft. Throw in the onion mixture, lime zest and a little salt and pepper. Toss gently then quickly transfer to warm plates.

4 Add a few drops of lime juice to each and a dusting of cayenne. Garnish the plates with two or three chives stalks each and serve straight away with warm French bread.

Turbot is a king amongst fish. It has meaty flesh with an exceptional flavour. I've coated it in a herby crumb coating and baked it quickly to ensure it remains moist and then served it with a piquant dressing. I like it with aubergine chips but you could serve French fries or plain boiled potatoes instead. This is great with halibut, too.

Herb-crusted turbot steaks with tomato, cucumber and anchovy

1 Mix the breadcrumbs with the fresh herbs and a little salt and pepper.

2 Dip the fish in the egg then the herb crust.

3 Heat the oil in a frying pan, add the fish and cook for about 3 minutes until golden underneath. Carefully turn the fish over and cook for a further 3 minutes until crisp and golden all over. Remove with a fish slice and drain on kitchen paper.

4 Meanwhile, put all the dressing ingredients in a saucepan and heat through gently. Season to taste.

5 Transfer the fish to warm plates. Spoon the dressing around and serve with Aubergine Chips and a green salad.

Serves 4

For the fish:
50 g fresh breadcrumbs
1 tbsp chopped fresh parsley
1 tbsp snipped fresh chives
1 tbsp chopped fresh thyme
Salt and freshly ground black pepper
4 turbot steaks (about 175 g each)
1 egg, beaten
Corn oil for shallow-frying
For the dressing:
6 tbsp olive oil
1 tbsp lemon juice
2.5 cm piece of cucumber, peeled and finely chopped
2 tomatoes, finely chopped
8 stoned black olives, finely chopped
2 canned anchovy fillets, finely chopped
1 garlic clove, crushed
1 tsp snipped fresh chives
To serve:
Aubergine Chips (see page 122) and a green salad

September

I like to serve this with quince jelly. To make about 1 kg, peel and chop about 900 g of quinces and put in a saucepan with just enough water to cover. Simmer for about 1½ hours until very soft. Strain through a jelly bag. Add 450 g of sugar to every 600 ml of juice plus the juice of a lemon. Heat until melted then boil until setting point is reached.

Guinea fowl with bread sauce and sage gravy on mangetout

Serves 4

1 oven-ready guinea fowl
1 onion, halved
6 fresh sage leaves
A large knob of butter
Salt and freshly ground black
  pepper
For the bread sauce:
2 slices of wholemeal bread
1 tsp grated onion
A good pinch each of ground cloves
  and grated nutmeg
200 ml milk
2 tbsp single cream
To finish:
225 g mangetout
3 tbsp plain flour
300 ml chicken stock, ideally fresh
  or made with 1 stock cube
1 tbsp soy sauce
To serve:
Roast potatoes and quince or
  redcurrant jelly

1 Pull out any fat from either side of the body cavity of the guinea fowl. Push the onion and two of the sage leaves into the cavity. Finely chop the rest of the sage and reserve. Smear the skin with the butter then sprinkle it with a little salt. Place in a roasting tin. Cover with foil or a lid and roast in a preheated oven at 190°C/gas 5/fan oven 170°C for 1½ hours.

2 Break the bread into small pieces. Put in a small ovenproof dish with the grated onion, spices and milk. Stir in a little salt and pepper and cover with a piece of buttered greaseproof paper. Cover with a lid or foil and cook in the oven for 1 hour. Remove from the oven, beat well with a fork to break up the bread, then stir in the cream. Taste and re-season.

3 When the bird is nearly ready, cook the mangetout in a little boiling, lightly salted water or steam them for 3–4 minutes until just tender but still bright green. Drain if necessary.

4 Transfer the guinea fowl to a carving dish. Stir the flour into the juices in the tin. Cook, stirring, for 2 minutes until lightly browned. Add the stock, chopped sage and soy sauce, bring to the boil and boil rapidly, stirring, for 2 minutes. Season to taste.

5 Cut the guinea fowl in quarters. Pile the mangetout on to four warm serving plates. Top each with a quarter of guinea fowl. Spoon the gravy over and put a spoonful of the bread sauce to one side. Serve with roast potatoes and quince or redcurrant jelly.

This rich beef casserole contains a lovely mix of vegetables. It takes on a Mediterranean feel with the addition of tomatoes, wine and olives. You may think it odd to have anchovies with beef. They melt as they cook to impart an amazing richness and depth of flavour to the sauce – not fishy at all!

Rich beef casserole with butternut squash and peppers

1 Heat half the oil in a large flameproof casserole. Add the onion and fry quickly for 2 minutes until lightly golden. Remove with a draining spoon.

2 Heat the remaining oil and fry the beef and lardons quickly on all sides to brown. Return the onion to the casserole.

3 Add all the prepared vegetables, the can of tomatoes, stock, wine, tomato purée, anchovies and bouquet garni. Stir well, adding the sugar and a little salt and pepper. Bring to the boil, then transfer to a preheated oven at 160°C/gas 3/fan oven 145°C; cook for 2 hours.

4 Stir in the wild mushrooms and olives. Return to the oven and cook for a further 30 minutes until the beef is really tender. Discard the bouquet garni, taste and re-season, if necessary. Sprinkle with the chopped parsley and serve with creamed potatoes.

Serves 4

2 tbsp olive oil
1 onion, chopped
700 g braising steak, cubed
50 g smoked lardons (diced bacon)
1 red pepper, diced
1 green pepper, diced
1 small butternut squash, diced
1 celery stick, diced
1 carrot, diced
1 garlic clove, crushed
400 g can of chopped tomatoes
300 ml beef stock
150 ml red wine
1 tbsp tomato purée
4 canned anchovy fillets, drained and chopped
1 bouquet garni sachet
A good pinch of caster sugar
Salt and freshly ground black pepper
100 g wild mushrooms, sliced
50 g stoned black olives
1 tbsp chopped fresh parsley

Aubergine chips have a gorgeous, creamy, sweet flavour that goes really well with fish, chicken or steak. They make a lovely change from potato fries. Try them, too, with any of the salsas or dipping sauces given in the book, particularly the avocado and soured cream one that goes with the potato skins on page 128.

Aubergine chips

Serves 4

2 aubergines
Salt
4 tbsp plain flour
Freshly ground black pepper
Sunflower or corn oil, for frying
Coarse sea salt

1 Cut the aubergines in thick slices then into fingers. Sprinkle with salt in a colander and leave to stand for 15 minutes. Rinse then dry well on kitchen paper. Toss in the flour seasoned with a little salt and pepper.

2 Heat 2.5 cm sunflower or corn oil in a large, heavy-based frying pan until a cube of day-old bread browns in 30 seconds. Lower the chips into the pan using a fish slice or draining spoon. Spread out evenly and fry quickly for 3–4 minutes until golden brown and tender.

3 Remove with the fish slice or draining spoon and drain on kitchen paper. Tip into a warm serving dish, sprinkle with coarse sea salt and serve hot.

This is a delightfully unusual way to serve marrow and is equally good made with courgettes. I like it best with grilled pork chops but you could also serve it with lamb or chicken, too. For vegetarians, you could add a drained can of chick peas and serve it over noodles.

Marrow with tomatoes, paprika and caraway

1 Peel the marrow, cut in quarters, remove the seeds and cut in bite-sized chunks.

2 Melt the butter in a saucepan, add the onion and fry gently for 1 minute. Add the marrow and fry, stirring, for 4–5 minutes until almost cooked.

3 Stir in the cherry tomatoes, paprika, half the caraway, the balsamic condiment and some salt and pepper. Cover the pan and cook gently for a further 3 minutes until the marrow is just tender and the tomatoes are cooked but still hold their shape.

4 Turn into a serving dish, top with the soured cream and sprinkle with the remaining caraway seeds.

Serves 4

1 young marrow
50 g unsalted butter
1 onion, finely chopped
225 g cherry tomatoes, halved
1 tbsp paprika
1 tsp caraway seeds
2 tbsp white balsamic condiment
Salt and freshly ground black pepper
2 tbsp soured cream

Blackberries have long been bedfellows with apples but the addition of elderberries adds a new dimension. The easiest way to remove the tiny berries from the stalks is to use the prongs of a fork. This flan is a lovely twist on the more usual blackberry and apple crumble.

Blackberry, apple and elderberry crumble flan

September

Serves 4

For the filling:
2 Bramley cooking apples, peeled, quartered, cored and thinly sliced
100 g blackberries
4 heads of elderberries, removed from their stalks
2 tbsp apple juice
Caster sugar, to taste
2 tsp cornflour
1 tbsp water
For the pastry:
75 g wholemeal flour
75 g plain flour
A pinch of salt
75 g butter, cut in cubes
75 g caster sugar
Cold water, to mix
2 tsp sifted icing sugar, for decorating
To serve:
Pouring cream

1 Put the apples, blackberries and elderberries in a pan. Add the apple juice and heat gently until the juices run, then simmer for about 5 minutes until just tender but the fruit still has some shape. Sweeten to taste with caster sugar.

2 Blend the cornflour with the water. Stir into the fruit and bring to the boil, stirring until thickened. Leave to cool while making the pastry.

3 Mix the flours with the salt in a bowl. Add the butter and rub in with the fingertips until the mixture resembles breadcrumbs. Stir in the 75 g of caster sugar.

4 Take out 4 heaped tablespoonfuls and reserve. Mix the remainder with enough cold water to form a firm dough. Knead gently on a lightly floured surface. Roll out and use to line an 18 cm flan dish. Stand the dish on a baking sheet.

5 Spoon the fruit into the dish and scatter the reserved crumble mixture over it.

6 Bake in a preheated oven at 190°C/gas 5/fan oven 170°C for about 30 minutes until golden.

7 Dust the top with icing sugar and serve with pouring cream.

To grind fresh hazelnuts, ideally, use a clean coffee grinder. Alternatively, use a blender or food processor but you'll have to stop the machine and scrape down the sides from time to time to process them all. This is a lovely dessert which you could serve with the last of the late-cropping raspberries.

Fresh cream hazelnut bavarois

1 Beat the egg yolks and sugar into the ground hazelnuts.

2 Bring the milk almost to the boil in a heavy non-stick pan. Pour over the egg, nut and sugar mixture, whisking all the time.

3 Pour back into the saucepan and cook over a very gentle heat, stirring all the time until the mixture coats the back of a spoon. Do not allow to boil or it will curdle. It will take a little time, so be patient.

4 Meanwhile, mix the gelatine with the water and leave to soften for 5 minutes. Then either stand the bowl in a pan of gently simmering water and stir until dissolved or heat briefly in the microwave. Again, do not allow to boil.

5 Stir the dissolved gelatine into the custard. Leave to cool, then chill until the consistency of egg white.

6 Whip the cream with the vanilla essence until softly peaking. Fold into the cold, almost-set custard with a metal spoon. Turn into four lightly oiled ramekin dishes (or one larger dish). Chill until set.

7 Loosen the edges and turn the bavarois out on to small serving plates (leave a large one in the dish). Trickle a little cream around the edges of the plates and add a cluster of three hazelnuts on the side.

Serves 4

2 egg yolks
40 g caster sugar
75 g ground hazelnuts
200 ml milk
1 tbsp powdered gelatine
1 tbsp water
300 ml double cream, plus extra for decorating
A few drops of vanilla essence
12 whole shelled hazelnuts

The heart of autumn with **apples** and **pears** at their peak, **pumpkins**, **marrows** and other **squashes** grown to perfection. The root crops are good, too, with **carrots**, **swedes**, **beetroot**, **turnips** and **yams** all in abundance. **Chestnuts**, **walnuts** and **quinces** are all ready this month and it's the game season for **pheasant**, **partridge**, **snipe**, **wild duck** and **grouse**. You'll still find some courgettes around but they are past their best, as are home-grown lettuces. **Jerusalem artichokes** may appear late in the month but are really in season from November. This is the time for good, meaty **eels**, too. I love them grilled on a late-in-the-year barbecue.

October

Vegetables

Aubergines, *beetroot, broccoli, butternut squash, cardoons, carrots, cavolo nero, celeriac, celery, chillies, curly kale, Florence fennel,* globe artichokes, *kohlrabi,* leeks, lettuces, *marrows,* onions, *peppers, potatoes (old, maincrop), pumpkins,* radishes, *rocket, swedes,* Swiss chard, *turnips,* watercress, wild mushrooms (blewits, ceps, chanterelles, field, horse, oyster, parasol, puffballs), *yams*

Fruit and nuts

Apples (Russets, Cox's, Bramleys), avocados (Hass), *chestnuts, damsons, figs, grapes,* hazelnuts, pawpaws, *pears (Comice, Conference), quinces, raspberries (late crop), tomatoes, walnuts*

Meat, poultry and game

Duck, goose, grouse, guinea fowl, hare, lamb, *partridge, pheasant, rabbit, snipe,* venison, *wild duck (mallard),* woodcock, *wood pigeon*

Fish and seafood

Bream, brill, brown shrimps, clams, *crabs,* Dublin Bay prawns (scampi), *eels,* grey mullet, haddock, hake, halibut, John Dory, lemon sole, *lobster, mackerel,* monkfish, *mussels, oysters,* plaice, *river trout (brown, rainbow), scallops, sea bass, squid, turbot*

Foods in season

Foods in *italics* are foods from the UK at the peak of their season.

Don't waste the scooped out potato. I mash it with a drained 185 g can of tuna, a tablespoonful of red or green Thai curry paste and a beaten egg, then shape the mix into cakes, coat in dried breadcrumbs and fry until golden for delicious fish cakes. Alternatively, mash it with a little butter and use it to top a shepherd's pie.

Spiced potato skins with soured cream and avocado salsa

Serves 4

8 potatoes, scrubbed and pricked
   all over with a fork
Corn oil for deep-frying
1 tsp ground cumin
½ tsp ground cinnamon
½ tsp onion salt
For the salsa:
1 avocado
2 tsp lemon juice
1 green pepper, finely diced
1 green chilli, seeded and chopped
1 spring onion, finely chopped
150 ml soured cream
A few drops of Worcestershire
   sauce
Salt and freshly ground black
   pepper

1 Push two potatoes on to each of four metal skewers so they go right through the potatoes. Bake in a preheated oven at 200°C/gas 6/fan oven 180°C for about 50 minutes until soft when squeezed.

2 Pull off the skewers. Cut in halves and scoop out most of the potato, leaving a 5 mm thick shell. Cut the skin halves into three wedges.

3 Heat the oil until a cube of day-old bread browns in 30 seconds. Deep-fry the skins for about 3 minutes until crisp and golden.

4 Drain on kitchen paper and tip into a bowl.

5 Mix the spices and onion salt together, sprinkle over the skins and toss gently to coat.

6 While the potatoes are baking, make the salsa. Halve the avocado, remove the stone and skin and finely dice the flesh. Put in a bowl. Toss in the lemon juice to prevent browning.

7 Add the pepper, chilli, spring onion and soured cream. Mix well and season to taste with the Worcestershire sauce, salt and pepper. Spoon into a small serving dish, then chill until ready to serve with the potato skins.

If you prefer you can use other blue cheeses, Cheddar or even a soft cheese like a ripe Brie instead of the Stilton. Freshly shelled walnuts are creamier in texture and less bitter than their pre-packed counterparts but, of course, you can use bought ones if fresh aren't available.

Warm Stilton and celery mousse with walnut dressing

1 Grease four ramekin dishes and line the bases with circles of non-stick baking parchment.

2 Mix the celery with the breadcrumbs and cheese. Beat the egg yolks with the cream and stir into the cheese mixture with the chives and a little salt and pepper.

3 Whisk the egg whites until stiff and fold in with a metal spoon. Turn into the prepared ramekins.

4 Stand the dishes in a frying pan with enough hot water to come half-way up the sides of the dishes. Cover with a lid or foil and cook over a very gentle heat for 20 minutes until set.

5 Whisk the oils with the condiment, a little salt and pepper and the chopped nuts.

6 Carefully loosen the edges of the mousses and turn out on to small plates. Spoon a little dressing around and garnish each mousse with two chives, cut in halves and put in a criss-cross pattern on the top.

Serves 4

2 tender inner celery sticks, very finely chopped
50 g soft white breadcrumbs
50 g Stilton cheese, crumbled
2 eggs, separated
120 ml single cream
2 tbsp snipped fresh chives
Salt and freshly ground black pepper
For the dressing:
4 tbsp olive oil, plus extra for greasing
1 tbsp walnut oil
2 tbsp white balsamic condiment
50 g shelled walnuts, finely chopped
8 chive stalks, for garnishing

Sun-blushed tomatoes are semi-dried and full of flavour. They also make a great antipasto with some sliced salami and Mozzarella. If you can only find baby squid, use 8–12 instead of the larger ones. I buy olives stuffed with anchovies in cans. Store the rest in a sealed container in the fridge (they won't last long!).

Pan-stewed squid with tomatoes and anchovy-stuffed olives

Serves 4

4 largish cleaned squid
120 ml olive oil
1 onion, very finely chopped
2 garlic cloves, crushed
2 tbsp chopped fresh parsley, plus a
little extra for garnishing
1 tbsp chopped fresh thyme
Salt and freshly ground black
pepper
1 lemon
25 g anchovy-stuffed olives, sliced
25 g sun-blushed tomatoes,
roughly chopped
To serve:
Crusty bread and a green salad

1 Rinse the squid and pat dry on kitchen paper. Chop the tentacles, discarding the hard core in the centre.

2 Heat the oil in a large pan. Add the onion and garlic and cook over a gentle heat, stirring, for 2 minutes to soften.

3 Add the squid, herbs and a little salt and pepper. Cut the lemon in half lengthways and squeeze the juice into the pan. Cover and cook gently for 20 minutes until the squid is tender, turning once.

4 Throw the olives and tomatoes into the pan and cook for a further minute. Taste and re-season if necessary.

5 Transfer to warm plates, sprinkle with a little extra chopped parsley and serve hot with lots of crusty bread and followed by a green salad.

When I had this as a child, my mother used to chop the eel into pieces and we ate it off the bone with our fingers. Here I've filleted the eel first but the choice is yours. If you buy the eels from a fishmonger, you could ask him to skin and fillet them for you as it's a bit fiddly.

Sautéed eels with beetroot and celeriac salad

1 Peel the vegetables, cut into bite-size chunks and shred in a food processor. Alternatively, cut into very fine matchsticks.

2 Mix with the olive oil, vinegar, sugar and some salt and pepper, then chill.

3 To skin and fillet the eels, make a cut all round just behind the head. Using a knife, ease the skin away a bit so you can get a grip on it. Dip your fingers in salt and, holding the head firmly with a damp cloth in one hand, tug off the skin with the other. It will come off in one but you need to use some brute force!

4 Cut off the head. Using a sharp filleting knife, make a cut along the backbone just above the line of bones. Ease the knife in at the head end then, holding the fish on top firmly with the other hand, slide the knife along the length of the eel to cut off the fillet. Turn the eel over and repeat on the other side. Cut the fillets into large diagonal chunks.

5 Mix the flour with the cumin, paprika, oregano and a little salt and pepper. Add the eel pieces and toss to coat.

6 Heat the sunflower oil in a large frying pan and fry the eel pieces for 3–4 minutes, tossing and turning until golden and cooked through. Drain on kitchen paper. Tip on to plates, put a pile of the salad to one side and a spoonful of soured cream. Serve with boiled potatoes.

Serves 4

For the salad:
2 raw beetroot
1 small onion
1/2 small celeriac
3 tbsp olive oil
1 tbsp balsamic vinegar
A good pinch of light brown sugar
Salt and freshly ground black pepper
For the eels:
2 good-sized freshwater eels
3 tbsp plain flour
1/2 tsp ground cumin
1 tsp paprika
1 tsp dried oregano
4 tbsp sunflower oil
To serve:
Soured cream and plain boiled potatoes

This is a traditionally British way of serving marrow. It's very easy but very tasty. You could add extra flavours, like tomato purée and a little chilli powder – even some red kidney beans to make the filling more like a chilli con carne but, to me, the excellence lies in its simplicity. Cook the potatoes at the same time as the marrow.

Stuffed marrow with rich onion gravy

Serves 4

4 onions
350 g minced beef
2 carrots, grated
600 ml beef stock, ideally fresh or made with 1 stock cube
1 bay leaf
Salt and freshly ground black pepper
1 marrow, peeled and cut into 8 slices
1 egg, beaten
50 g Cheddar cheese, grated
15 g butter, plus extra for greasing
1 tsp caster sugar
3 tbsp plain flour
1 tbsp chopped fresh parsley, for garnishing
To serve:
Jacket-baked potatoes

1. Chop one of the onions, thinly shred the other three. Put the chopped onion in a pan with the beef and carrots. Fry, stirring, until the grains of meat are separate and no longer pink.

2. Add 300 ml of the stock, the bay leaf and a little salt and pepper. Bring to the boil, then simmer for 5 minutes. Discard the bay leaf and drain off any liquid into the rest of the stock.

3. Meanwhile, peel the marrow, cut into eight and scoop out the seeds. Arrange in a single layer in a lightly buttered baking dish.

4. Beat the egg into the mince. Spoon into the marrow. Cover with the grated cheese. Cover the dish loosely with buttered foil (so it doesn't touch the cheese) and bake in a preheated oven at 190°C/gas 5/fan oven 170°C for 40 minutes. Remove the foil and cook for a further 10 minutes to brown the top.

5. Meanwhile, make the gravy. Melt the butter in a heavy-based saucepan. Add the onions and fry, stirring, for 3 minutes. Add the sugar and continue to fry the onions for 5 minutes, stirring, until a rich golden brown. Blend in the flour then the remaining stock. Bring to the boil, stirring, and cook for 2 minutes until thickened and smooth. Season to taste.

6. Transfer the marrow to warm plates. Spoon the gravy around and sprinkle with parsley. Serve with jacket-baked potatoes.

The duck is marinated in soy sauce and garlic then quickly fried and served with a fruity damson sauce, flavoured with hoisin, honey and fresh ginger. It's served on a bed of rice with stir-fried vegetables for a complete, very colourful dish. You could use 4–8 plums (depending on their size), instead of the damsons, when in season.

Crispy duck breasts with damson and ginger sauce

1 Score the duck skin in a criss-cross pattern. Mix 1 tbsp of the soy sauce with the garlic. Rub all over the duck, especially into the slits in the skin. Leave to marinate for at least 1 hour.

2 Cook the rice in plenty of boiling, lightly salted water for 10 minutes or until just tender but still with some 'bite'. Drain, rinse with boiling water and drain again.

3 Heat 1 tbsp of the oil in a saucepan. Add the spring onions and fry, stirring, for 2 minutes. Add the damsons and cook, stirring, until the juices run. Add the ginger, hoisin sauce, 1 tbsp of the remaining soy sauce and the honey. Cover and cook gently for 4 minutes. Remove from the heat.

4 Fry the duck breasts, skin-sides down, in a non-stick frying pan for 4 minutes until the fat runs and the skin is crispy and golden brown. Turn over and fry for a further 3 minutes. Remove from the pan and keep warm.

5 Heat the remaining oil with the duck juices and add the prepared vegetables. Stir-fry for 4 minutes. Add the remaining soy sauce and the rice and toss for 1 minute.

6 Pile the vegetables and rice on to four plates. Carve the duck breasts into diagonal slices and re-form on top. Reheat the sauce and spoon over.

Serves 4

4 duck breasts with skin
3 tbsp soy sauce
1 garlic clove, crushed
225 g long-grain rice
2 tbsp sunflower oil
1 bunch of spring onions, chopped
12 ripe damsons, stoned and chopped
1 tsp of grated fresh root ginger
4 tbsp hoisin sauce
2 tsp clear honey
2 celery sticks, cut in matchsticks
2 carrots, cut in matchsticks
1 red and 1 green pepper, cut in thin strips
2 turnips, cut in matchsticks

This is one of my favourite ways of serving big, open field mushrooms. The flavour is just out of this world. I recommend lots of crusty bread to mop up the juices. If you can't find field mushrooms, you can use home-grown, organic, open cultivated ones. The flavour won't be quite as good but they're still worth cooking.

Field mushrooms with garlic and cider

Serves 4

25 g butter
8–12 large, flat field mushrooms, peeled and stalks removed
2 large garlic cloves, finely chopped
150 ml dry cider
150 ml crème fraîche
Salt and freshly ground black pepper
2 tbsp chopped fresh parsley

1 Smear a large roasting tin with the butter. Lay the mushrooms in the tin.

2 Chop the stalks and scatter over the top with the garlic.

3 Pour the cider over. Season well.

4 Cover with foil and bake in a preheated oven at 190°C/gas 5/fan oven 170°C for 20 minutes.

5 Carefully lift out the mushrooms with a fish slice and transfer to warm, shallow dishes. Keep warm. Blend the crème fraîche into the juices and bring to the boil on the hob. Allow to bubble for a few minutes to thicken slightly. Taste and re-season if necessary.

6 Spoon over the mushrooms and sprinkle with parsley.

You can enjoy a plethora of vegetables served golden-roasted but with their own colours shining through. They look much more exciting than plain potatoes, taste divine and are a lovely accompaniment to any roasted meat or poultry. Ring the changes with whatever root vegetables you have to hand.

Mixed roasted roots with mint and coarse sea salt

1 Peel all the vegetables and cut in walnut-sized chunks. Keep the beetroot separate.

2 Toss each set of vegetables in a little of the oil. Spread out in a large roasting tin, keeping the beetroot as separate from the other vegetables as you can.

3 Roast in a preheated oven at 200°C /gas 6/fan oven 180°C for about 45 minutes or until tender and golden, turning once.

4 Now mix the vegetables together, sprinkle with the mint and coarse sea salt and serve very hot.

Serves 4

$1/2$ celeriac
1 kohlrabi
1 yam
$1/2$ small swede
1 large beetroot
3 tbsp olive oil
1 tbsp chopped fresh mint
1 tsp coarse sea salt

Figs are quite expensive to buy in supermarkets so unless you have your own tree or know someone who has one, look out for them in a farmer's market or at a local growers. Actually, you could get away with serving only one fig each but it wouldn't look very generous!

Grilled goats' cheese with fresh figs in port

Serves 4

120 ml port
120 ml red grape juice
50 g soft light brown sugar
1 piece of cinnamon stick
3 cloves
1 star anise
1 lime, sliced
8 –12 fresh figs
4 x 70 g discs of goats' cheese
1 tbsp sunflower oil
2 tbsp icing sugar, for dusting
To serve:
Digestive or other semi-sweet
   wheatmeal biscuits

1 Put the port and grape juice in a frying pan with the sugar, spices and lime slices. Stir over a gentle heat until the sugar dissolves.

2 Add the figs and simmer gently for about 15 minutes, turning over once or twice in the liquid until the fruit has taken on the colour of the liquid and is tender.

3 Carefully lift the fruit out of the liquid and place in a plastic container with a lid.

4 Boil the juice rapidly for a few minutes until syrupy. Pour over the figs, cover and leave to cool, then chill.

5 When ready to serve, spoon the figs to one side of four small serving plates with a trickle of juice. Brush the cheeses with the oil and place on foil on a grill rack. Cook under a preheated grill for 2 minutes until melting slightly and turning lightly golden.

6 Quickly transfer to the plates and dust with a little sifted icing sugar. Serve straight away with digestive or other semi-sweet wheatmeal biscuits.

I hate having stones in my food when I eat it, so I always remove them before cooking. However, you can cook the fruit whole and let everyone take out their own as they eat their pudding. This dessert is also delicious with Victoria plums or greengages, when in season, instead of the damsons.

Autumn damson and almond crumble

1 Put the damsons in a saucepan with the orange zest and juice and 50 g of the sugar. Heat gently until the sugar dissolves then cover and cook over a gentle heat for 5 minutes only, until the juices are running and the fruit is nearly tender but still in neat pieces.

2 Turn into an ovenproof serving dish and scatter the flaked almonds over.

3 Mix the flour with the ground almonds. Add the butter and rub in with the fingertips until the mixture resembles breadcrumbs.

4 Stir in the remaining sugar. Spoon over the damsons and press down firmly.

5 Bake in a preheated oven at 190°C/gas 5/fan oven 170°C for about 40 minutes until golden on top and the damsons are tender.

6 Serve warm with custard.

Serves 4

450 g damsons, halved and stoned, if liked
Finely grated zest and juice of 1 orange
100 g caster sugar
50 g flaked almonds
75 g plain flour
40 g ground almonds
50 g butter, cut in small pieces
To serve:
Custard

Roots and **greens** are the order of the day. You'll still find some **wild mushrooms** and **late-crop raspberries**, which are lovely treats. **Squashes** and **pumpkins** are good – many people seem to ignore them once Halloween is over! It's also the **white truffle** season. If you can buy a small amount, grate it over an omelette or a simple risotto – the flavour is out of this world and worth the price. **Sloes** are ready too so make sloe gin. Prick about 225 g of them with a darning needle, put them in an empty gin bottle, add 175 g of granulated sugar, a few drops of natural almond essence and 4 juniper berries and top up with gin. Screw on the cap and shake gently until the sugar dissolves. Store in a cool, dark place for three months. Strain out the sloes and re-bottle the gin. Use the fruit in a fruit salad or with ice-cream.

November

Vegetables

Beetroot, butternut squash, cabbages (green, red, white), cardoons, carrots, cavolo nero, celeriac, celery, chicory, curly kale, Jerusalem artichokes, kohlrabi, leeks, lettuces, *parsnips, potatoes (old, maincrop), pumpkins, salsify and scorzonera, shallots, swedes,* Swiss chard, *turnips,* watercress, white truffles, *wild mushrooms (blewits, horse, oyster)*

Fruit and nuts

Apples (Russets, Cox's, Bramleys), avocados (Fuerte, Hass), *chestnuts,* cranberries, dates, *medlars,* pears (Comice, Conference), persimmons, *quinces, raspberries (late crop), sloes, walnuts*

Meat, poultry and game

Duck, *goose, grouse, guinea fowl, hare, partridge, pheasant, rabbit, snipe, venison,* woodcock, *wood pigeon*

Fish and seafood

Bream, brill, clams, *cod, crabs,* Dublin Bay prawns (scampi), *haddock,* hake, halibut, John Dory, lemon sole, *lobster,* monkfish, *mussels, oysters,* plaice, *scallops, sea bass, squid,* turbot

Foods in season

Foods in *italics* are foods from the UK at the peak of their season.

This hearty soup smacks of Tuscany in Italy – white beans, black cabbage, garlic, tomatoes and white wine, simmered together to make a memorable meal with lots of crusty bread. If you need anything afterwards, I'd choose some good cheeses, more bread and celery.

White bean soup with cavolo nero

Serves 4

1 tbsp olive oil
1 onion, finely chopped
1 garlic clove, crushed
2 celery sticks, finely chopped
1 carrot, finely chopped
600 ml vegetable or chicken stock, ideally fresh or made with 1 stock cube
6 tbsp dry white wine
400 g can of chopped tomatoes
425 g can of haricot beans, drained
1 tbsp tomato purée
A good pinch of caster sugar
1 bouquet garni sachet
1 small head of cavolo nero, finely shredded
Salt and freshly ground black pepper
To serve:
Grated fresh Parmesan cheese and crusty bread

1 Heat the oil in a large saucepan. Add the onion, garlic, celery and carrot and cook gently, stirring, for 2 minutes until softened but not browned.

2 Add the remaining ingredients and simmer for 25 minutes. Discard the bouquet garni. Taste and re-season, if necessary.

3 Ladle the soup into warm bowls and serve with grated fresh Parmesan cheese and crusty bread.

You can use other squashes or even courgettes for a change from pumpkin in this delicate but sumptuous dish. It makes a glamorous starter but is also ideal for a light lunch. I'd serve it with a side salad too, for a completely balanced meal. As you need only a few chestnuts, it's not such an effort to prepare them yourself.

Spiced pumpkin custards with date and chestnut salpiçon

1 Peel, seed and dice the pumpkin. Put it in a saucepan with the leek. Add the water. Cover and cook fairly gently for about 10 minutes until very soft and the liquid has been absorbed.

2 Purée in a blender or food processor with the cumin, eggs and cream. Season to taste.

3 Spoon the mixture into four individual ramekin dishes. Place in a frying pan with enough hot water to come half way up the sides of the dishes. Cover and cook over a very gentle heat for 20 minutes or until set.

4 Meanwhile, make the salpiçon. Mix the dates with the chestnuts, oil, vinegar, honey and parsley and heat gently in a saucepan.

5 Transfer the dishes of custard to individual plates and allow to cool for 5 minutes. Top each with a spoonful of the salpiçon. Serve with warm bagels.

Serves 4

500 g pumpkin
1 leek, thinly sliced
120 ml water
1 tsp cumin
2 eggs
284 ml carton single cream
Salt and freshly ground black
   pepper
For the salpiçon:
4 fresh dates, stoned and chopped
4 cooked chestnuts (see page 158),
   peeled, skinned and chopped
2 tbsp olive oil
1 tsp red wine vinegar
1 tsp clear honey
1 tbsp chopped fresh parsley
To serve:
Warm bagels

Fish pie is a traditional favourite in this country. Here I've used lovely meaty cod in a creamy sauce with sautéed leeks and mushrooms. It's topped with fluffy mashed potatoes then smothered in Red Leicester cheese before baking to golden perfection. It only needs some peas and carrots as an accompaniment.

Leicester creamed cod and leek pie

Serves 4

700 g potatoes, cut in small chunks
400 ml milk
25 g butter
700 g cod fillet, skinned
1 bay leaf
Salt and freshly ground black
   pepper
2 leeks, thinly sliced
50 g button mushrooms, sliced
25 g plain flour
60 ml single cream
50 g Red Leicester cheese, grated

1 Cook the potatoes in boiling, lightly salted water for about 10 minutes or until tender. Drain and mash thoroughly with 2 tbsp of the milk and a knob of the butter.

2 Meanwhile, cook the fish in the remaining milk with the bay leaf and a little salt and pepper for about 5 minutes until the fish flakes easily with a fork. Carefully lift out of the milk and flake, discarding any bones.

3 Melt the remaining butter in a saucepan and gently fry the leeks and mushrooms for 2 minutes, stirring. Blend in the flour then remove from the heat and whisk in the fish milk (discarding the bay leaf). Bring to the boil, stirring until thick. Stir in the cream and fish. Taste and re-season.

4 Turn the mixture into a flameproof dish. Pile the potato on top, spreading it out and roughing it up with a fork. Scatter the cheese over.

5 Cook under a preheated grill for about 5 minutes or until golden and bubbling. Serve hot.

This is based on a dish I had in Provence several years ago. There they used peppers and courgettes but, as I want to use seasonal foods, I've made it with butternut squash, celery and leeks with canned pimientos. The result is fabulous both in flavour and colour. Use other seafood when in season.

Provençal mixed seafood stew

1 Scrub the mussels and discard the 'beards'. Throw away any that are broken, open or don't close when tapped sharply with a knife.

2 Fry the onion, garlic and celery in the oil for 2 minutes, stirring, until softened but not browned.

3 Add the vinegar, wine, water, tomatoes, sugar, leeks, squash and a little salt and pepper. Bring to the boil, part-cover and simmer for 8 minutes.

4 Add the pimientos, herbs, cod, squid and mussels. Bring back to the boil, cover and cook for a further 5 minutes until the fish is cooked and the mussels have opened. Discard any mussels that remain shut.

5 Stir gently, ladle into warm bowls, sprinkle with parsley, add a lemon wedge to the side of each bowl and serve with crusty bread.

Serves 4

900 g mussels
1 onion, chopped
2 garlic cloves, crushed
2 celery sticks, sliced
1 tbsp olive oil
2 tbsp white wine vinegar
300 ml dry white wine
300 ml water
400 g can of chopped tomatoes
1 tsp caster sugar
2 leeks, thinly sliced
1 butternut squash, diced
Salt and freshly ground black pepper
200 g can of pimientos, drained and chopped
$\frac{1}{2}$ tsp herbes de Provence
450 g cod, skinned and cubed
6 cleaned baby squid, sliced into rings and tentacles chopped
A little chopped fresh parsley and lemon wedges, for garnishing
To serve:
Crusty bread

All venison, whether farmed or wild, is free range and has the lowest fat content of any red meat and a wonderful rich flavour. With this dish I like to serve shredded, lightly cooked Savoy cabbage but you may prefer beans, peas or another vegetable. Alternatively, serve a green salad afterwards to offset the richness.

Venison steaks in port and balsamic jus with parsnip mash

Serves 4

4 venison steaks
2 tbsp sunflower oil
6 tbsp port
4 tbsp apple juice
2 tbsp balsamic vinegar
½ tsp dried mixed herbs
Salt and freshly ground black pepper
2 large potatoes, cut in chunks
2 large parsnips, cut in chunks
1 tsp walnut oil
2 tbsp double cream
50 g shelled walnuts, chopped
40 g butter
3 tbsp redcurrant jelly
2 tsp tomato purée
2 tbsp chopped fresh parsley, for garnishing

1 Put the steaks in a dish. Mix the oil with the port, apple juice balsamic vinegar, herbs and a little salt and pepper and pour over the steaks. Leave to marinate for 3 hours, turning once or twice.

2 Cook the potatoes and parsnips together in boiling, lightly salted water for about 10 minutes or until tender. Drain, mash well with the walnut oil, cream, nuts and 15 g of the butter. Season to taste.

3 Meanwhile, melt the remaining butter in a frying pan. Lift the steaks out of the marinade and fry quickly on each side to brown. Turn down the heat and fry for 3 minutes on each side until just cooked and tender. Transfer to a plate and keep the steaks warm.

4 Stir the marinade into the frying pan with the redcurrant jelly and tomato purée. Bring to the boil and boil rapidly, stirring, until slightly reduced. Taste and re-season if necessary.

5 Pile the mash on to warm plates. Put the steaks to one side and spoon the sauce over. Garnish with chopped parsley and serve straight away.

Grouse is a lovely bird, full of flavour and not too tough! You can roast it like the guinea fowl on page 120 but I love it casseroled with some roots, wine and cream. You could use cider and two sliced Cox's apples instead of the mushrooms and wine. The result would be reminiscent of a classic Normandy dish.

Grouse with turnips, mushrooms and white wine

1 Melt 25 g of the butter in a flameproof casserole and brown the grouse on all sides. Remove from the casserole.

2 Add the onion and turnips and fry, stirring, for 2 minutes. Stir in the flour and cook for 1 minute, stirring all the time. Remove from the heat and blend in the stock and wine. Return to the heat and bring to the boil, stirring until thickened. Add the mushrooms.

3 Return the grouse to the pan, breasts down, pushing down well in the sauce. Add the bouquet garni and a little salt and pepper. Cover and cook in a preheated oven at 180°C/gas 4/fan oven 160°C for 1½ hours until really tender.

4 Carefully lift the grouse out of the pan and transfer to warm serving plates (the right way up!). Discard the bouquet garni. Stir the cream into the sauce and heat through. Taste and re-season if necessary.

5 Spoon the sauce over the birds and garnish with parsley. Serve with creamed potatoes and buttered cabbage.

Serves 4

40 g butter
2 oven-ready grouse, halved
1 large onion, chopped
4 turnips, diced
25 g plain flour
300 ml chicken stock, ideally fresh or made with 1 stock cube
300 ml medium-dry white wine
100 g baby button mushrooms, left whole
1 bouquet garni sachet
Salt and freshly ground black pepper
4 tbsp double cream
1 tbsp chopped fresh parsley, for garnishing
To serve:
Creamed potatoes and buttered cabbage

Okay, nachos should be made with corn tortilla chips but chicory makes a fabulous alternative as a receptacle for filling with refried or mashed beans and pickled chillies then topping with melted cheese to eat in your fingers as a snack! If you need extra crunch, you could crumble some tortillas over the beans before adding the cheese!

Red chicory 'nachos' with spicy beans

Serves 4

2 heads of red chicory
425 g can of pinto beans, drained
1 garlic clove, crushed
$\frac{1}{4}$ tsp chilli powder
Salt and freshly ground black
   pepper
1 tbsp pickled sliced jalapeño
   peppers, chopped
100 g Cheddar cheese, grated

1 Cut a cone shape out of the base of each head of chicory then separate into leaves. Arrange in a single layer on a large flameproof platter.

2 Thoroughly mash the beans with a fork. Mash in the garlic and chilli and season to taste.

3 Spoon the beans into the chicory leaves. Scatter the chopped pepper and grated cheese over.

4 Flash under a preheated grill for 2–3 minutes until the cheese melts and bubbles. Serve straight away.

This is a gorgeous side dish to serve with lamb or chicken casseroles or as a vegetarian dish, with some hummus, thinned with a little milk and heated as a sauce. You can vary it at other times of the year with courgettes, aubergines, peppers and, well, any vegetables you like!

Vegetable couscous with spices and fresh coriander

1 Melt the butter in a heavy-based saucepan. Add the onion and fry, stirring, for 2 minutes. Add the rest of the vegetables, a little seasoning and the spices, toss, then add the water.

2 Bring to the boil, cover, reduce the heat and cook very gently for about 15 minutes until the vegetables are really tender but still hold their shape.

3 Meanwhile, put the couscous in a bowl and stir in the vegetable stock. Leave to stand for 5 minutes until the liquid is absorbed. Stand the bowl over the saucepan of vegetables and cover with the lid. Leave to steam while the vegetables cook.

4 When the vegetables are cooked, they should have absorbed the liquid; if not, turn up the heat and cook quickly for a minute or two to evaporate it.

5 Add the vegetables to the couscous with the coriander and toss all together. Taste and re-season if necessary. Serve hot.

Serves 4

15 g butter
1 onion, sliced
1 garlic clove, crushed
2 turnips, diced
½ small swede, diced
1 small butternut squash, diced
Salt and freshly ground black pepper
1 tsp ground cumin
½ tsp ground cinnamon
½ tsp ground ginger
4 tbsp water
225 g couscous
600 ml vegetable stock, ideally fresh or made with 1 stock cube
2 tbsp chopped fresh coriander

What could be more British than apples and custard? Here custard nestles in a sweet, short-pastry case and is topped with English Cox's apples then baked in the oven until the apples are glazed and turning golden. I like to serve this tart with crème fraîche but you may prefer a spoonful of vanilla ice-cream.

Cox's apple and custard tart

Serves 6

For the pastry:
225 g plain flour
A pinch of salt
200 g butter, cubed
25 g caster sugar
1 egg yolk
For the filling:
2 tbsp cornflour
2 tbsp plain flour
4 tbsp caster sugar
300 ml milk
1 large egg
A few drops of vanilla essence
3–4 Cox's apples
1 tbsp lemon juice
25 g icing sugar

1. Make the pastry. Sift the flour and salt into a bowl. Add the butter and rub in with the fingertips. Stir in the caster sugar. Add the egg yolk and stir with a knife, then draw the mixture together into a ball with your hands. Wrap in clingfilm, then chill for 30 minutes.

2. Roll out and use to line a 23 cm flan dish. Prick the base with a fork and fill with crumpled foil. Bake in a preheated oven at 200°C/gas 6/fan oven 180°C for 10 minutes. Remove the foil and cook for a further 5 minutes to dry out.

3. Make the custard. Whisk the flours with the sugar and a little of the milk in a saucepan until smooth. Beat the egg with the remaining milk and strain into the pan. Add a few drops of vanilla essence. Whisking all the time, bring to the boil and cook for 2 minutes until the custard is thick and smooth. Turn into the flan case.

4. Peel, quarter, core and thinly slice the apples and toss in the lemon juice. Arrange attractively over the custard. Sift the icing sugar all over the surface.

5. Bake in the oven for 20–25 minutes or until the apples are tender and turning golden brown. Serve warm.

In the seventies, it was very trendy to make a dessert with gingernuts and cream, layered together. I got to thinking that it wasn't a bad concept so came up with the idea of Nice biscuits, soaked in brandy and sandwiched with a coffee and walnut filling and smothered in whipped cream. The coffee liqueur just rounds it off!

Coffee and walnut slice with liqueur trickle

1 Beat the butter with the milk and icing sugar then beat in the finely chopped walnuts and vanilla essence.

2 Mix the coffee granules with the water and brandy.

3 Dip a biscuit in the coffee mixture then spread with a little of the walnut mixture. Dip another biscuit and sandwich it to the first. Place them on a serving plate. Repeat until all the biscuits are sandwiched together in a line.

4 Whip the cream until stiffly peaking and spread all over the biscuit block. Decorate with the prongs of a fork. Chill.

5 To serve, cut the block in half lengthways, then into three or four slices, crossways. Tip the slices on their sides on serving plates (so you can see the layers). Trickle a spoonful of Tia Maria around each one.

Serves 6–8

50 g butter, softened
2 tsp milk
150 g icing sugar, sifted
75 g shelled walnuts, finely chopped
A few drops of vanilla essence
2 tsp instant coffee granules
5 tbsp hot water
1 tbsp brandy
250 g packet Nice biscuits
300 ml double cream
6–8 tsp Tia Maria or other coffee liqueur

November

Christmas is coming and the winter vegetables come to the fore: **carrots**, **Jerusalem artichokes**, **parsnips** and **swedes** are all in good supply. **Sprouts**, of course, are at their best – choose the baby ones for the sweetest flavour. If you want something a little crisper and fresher, go for **chicory** or **radicchio**. When I was a child, we used to have chicory for tea on a Sunday with bread and butter: the spears trickled with malt vinegar and pepper – delicious! **Goose**, **turkey** and **venison** are all at their peak in time for the festive season, and **almonds**, **chestnuts**, **dates** and **cranberries** are ready to please. Small citrus fruits like **tangerines** are excellent and will have the best flavour of the year. There's plenty of good **fish** available, especially **mussels** and **oysters**.

December

Vegetables

Beetroot, *brussels sprouts, cabbages (green, red, white)*, cardoons, *carrots*, cauliflowers, *celeriac, celery, chicory, curly kale, Jerusalem artichokes*, lettuces, *parsnips, potatoes (old, maincrop)*, pumpkins, *radicchio, shallots, swedes*, Swiss chard, *turnips*, watercress

Fruit and nuts

Almonds, *apples (Russets, Cox's, Bramleys)*, avocados (Fuerte), *chestnuts*, clementines, cranberries, dates, medlars, passion fruit, pears (Comice, Conference), physalis, pineapples, pomegranates, satsumas, tangerines, walnuts

Meat, poultry and game

Duck, *goose*, grouse, *guinea fowl, hare, partridge, pheasant*, rabbit, *snipe, turkey, venison*, wild duck (mallard), *woodcock, wood pigeon*

Fish and seafood

Bream, brill, clams, haddock, hake, halibut, John Dory, lemon sole, monkfish, *mussels, oysters*, plaice, scallops, *sea bass*, turbot

Foods in season

Foods in *italics* are foods from the UK at the peak of their season.

This silky smooth soup is enriched with cream and egg yolks and is one of my favourites for lunch or as a starter for a dinner party. The celery bits add cooling crunch to nibble with the soup but you can just add some croûtons (see page 116) at the last minute, if you prefer.

Creamed leek and celeriac soup with blue cheese celery bites

Serves 4

25 g butter
1 onion, chopped
½ celeriac, diced
2 large leeks, sliced
1 large potato, diced
1 litre chicken or vegetable stock, ideally fresh or made with 1 stock cube
1 bay leaf
Salt and freshly ground black pepper
4 tbsp dried milk powder
1 egg yolk
2 tbsp single cream
For the celery bites:
50 g Stilton or other blue cheese
15 g unsalted butter, softened
A pinch of cayenne
2 tender celery sticks
A few celery leaves and 1 tbsp chopped fresh parsley, for garnishing

1 Melt the butter in a saucepan. Add the prepared vegetables and cook, stirring, over a gentle heat for 3 minutes until slightly softened but not turning colour.

2 Add the stock, bay leaf and a little salt and pepper. Bring to the boil, reduce the heat, part-cover and simmer gently for 30 minutes until everything is really tender.

3 Discard the bay leaf. Purée in a blender or food processor with the milk powder, egg yolk and half the cream. Return to the saucepan.

4 Reheat very gently, stirring all the time, but do not allow to boil or even bubble. Taste and re-season.

5 Meanwhile, make the celery bites. Mash the cheese with the butter and cayenne. Spread it in the groove in the celery. Cut the sticks into short lengths, arrange on a serving plate. Garnish with a few celery leaves.

6 Ladle the soup into warm bowls and garnish with parsley. Hand the celery bites separately.

Oysters are a fiddle to shuck – or open – but the skill is to make sure you don't spill all the lovely juices from within the shell, so no sharp movements. You can buy a proper oyster knife if you have oysters more than once a year but an ordinary, small, pointed vegetable knife will do just as well.

Grilled oysters with crème fraîche and Parmesan crust

1 Shuck the oysters by holding one at a time firmly in an oven-gloved hand. Insert the sharp point of a knife between the two shells near the hinge. Push the knife against the hinge, twisting until the hinge breaks. Carefully open the oyster, taking care to keep all the juices intact. Loosen the oyster from the shell with the knife.

2 Drain off most of the juices and mix with the crème fraîche and some black pepper.

3 Put the oysters on a baking sheet. Spoon the crème fraîche mixture over.

4 Mix the breadcrumbs with the cheese, melted butter and cayenne. Sprinkle over the crème fraîche.

5 Cook under a hot pre-heated grill, fairly near the heat source, for 2–3 minutes until the tops are golden and bubbling. Serve straight away.

Serves 4–6

24 oysters
150 ml crème fraîche
Freshly ground black pepper
50 g fresh breadcrumbs
50 g Parmesan cheese, freshly grated
50 g butter, melted
A good pinch of cayenne

Halibut is a lovely fish with a fantastically moist texture and a wonderful flavour. Here I've browned the fish then cooked it gently on a bed of grated potatoes, onions and diced ham, smothered in cream. It makes a complete meal with just a side vegetable or you could serve a green salad instead.

Halibut with ham and potatoes in cream sauce

Serves 4

50 g butter
4 halibut steaks, about 150 g each
1 large onion, finely chopped
4 large potatoes, peeled and
  coarsely grated
100 g cooked ham, diced
300 ml double cream
3 tbsp chopped fresh parsley
Salt and freshly ground black
  pepper
To serve:
Carrots

1 Melt half the butter in a large frying pan. Add the halibut, skin-side up, and fry quickly for 3 minutes to brown. Remove from the pan.

2 Melt the remaining butter, add the onion and stir-fry for 2 minutes. Add the potatoes and toss until softening. Reduce the heat, cover and cook very gently for 5 minutes, stirring occasionally, until almost tender.

3 Stir in the ham, cream, 2 tbsp of the parsley and salt and pepper to taste. Put the fish on top, skin-side down. Cover and cook over a fairly gentle heat for 6–8 minutes until the fish is cooked through and the potato mixture is cooked and creamy.

4 Carefully lift off the fish. Spoon the potato mixture on to warm plates and put the fish on top. Sprinkle with the remaining chopped parsley and serve with carrots.

You can use any fresh fish fillets for this dish – trout and mackerel are almost as good as the sea bass when they are at their best. It's worth cooking the turnips and onions in a separate pan so they can cook until sweet and golden and can be dished up at the same time as the fish, which cooks in just a few minutes.

Pan-roasted sea bass, turnips and onions with caper dressing

1 Heat 1 tbsp of the oil with the butter in a frying pan. Add the turnips and onions and fry quickly until golden all over. Reduce the heat, cover and cook very gently, shaking the pan occasionally, for about 10 minutes until tender.

2 When the vegetables are nearly cooked, heat 2 tbsp of the remaining oil in a separate pan. Add the fillets, skin-side up, and fry for 1 minute.

3 Turn them over so the skin is down and cook for a further 3-4 minutes until cooked through and the skin underneath is golden.

4 Meanwhile, whisk the remaining oil with the rosemary, mustard, vinegar, sugar and capers. Season to taste.

5 Spoon the turnips and onions on to warm plates. Lay a fillet beside each, skin-side up, and spoon the dressing over. Serve with plain boiled or steamed potatoes and a green salad.

Serves 4

5 tbsp olive oil
25 g butter
8 baby turnips, peeled but left whole
12 baby onions, peeled but left whole
4 sea bass fillets, about 150 g each
1 tsp chopped fresh rosemary
$\frac{1}{2}$ tsp Dijon mustard
2 tbsp white wine vinegar
1 tsp caster sugar
2 tsp pickled capers
Salt and freshly ground black pepper
To serve:
Plain boiled or steamed potatoes and a green salad

Serve this lovely warm salad with crusty bread or with jacket-baked potatoes, either cooked in the oven or in the microwave. You could use leftover cooked turkey on Boxing Day (or the day after), in which case stir-fry the meat with all the vegetables for just 3–4 minutes until piping hot.

Warm turkey strip salad with radicchio and cranberries

Serves 4

8 tbsp olive oil
4 shallots, sliced
1 garlic clove, crushed
225 g turkey stir-fry meat
4 carrots, cut in thin matchsticks
175 g button mushrooms, sliced
2 heads of radicchio
2 Little Gem lettuce
6 fresh sage leaves, shredded
50 g fresh cranberries
4 tbsp cranberry juice drink
4 tbsp white balsamic condiment
1 tsp Dijon mustard
Salt and freshly ground black
  pepper

1 Heat 2 tbsp of the oil in a wok or frying pan. Add the shallots, garlic and turkey and stir-fry for 3 minutes.

2 Add the carrots and mushrooms and stir-fry for a further 3 minutes.

3 Separate the leaves of radicchio and lettuce and tear into pieces. Mix together and pile on plates. Spoon the turkey mixture over.

4 Quickly add the remaining oil, sage, the cranberries, juice drink, balsamic condiment and mustard to the pan juices and heat, stirring, for a few minutes until the cranberries pop. Season to taste.

5 Spoon over the turkey mixture and serve warm.

I haven't included muscatel raisins in the monthly lists because, being dried, they are, arguably, not seasonal but they appear to be more readily available at this time of year. This recipe is gorgeous made with a fruity white wine – like Mosel – but you could use medium-sweet cider instead.

Pheasant with muscatel raisins on artichoke and potato crush

1 Melt the butter in a flameproof casserole. Add the shallots and fry gently for a few minutes until browned all over. Remove from the pan with a draining spoon.

2 Add the lardons and mushrooms and fry, stirring, for 1 minute. Remove from the pan with a draining spoon.

3 Add the pheasant to the pan and fry until browned all over.

4 Return the shallots, lardons and mushrooms to the pan. Add the stock, wine and raisins. Bring to the boil and season to taste. Add the bay leaf.

5 Cover and transfer to a preheated oven at 180°C/gas 4/fan oven 160°C for 1 hour or until the pheasant is really tender.

6 Meanwhile, peel and cut the potatoes and artichokes into chunks. Put them immediately in cold water in a saucepan with the lemon juice. Bring to the boil, then boil for about 10 minutes or until tender.

7 Drain and roughly crush. Stir in the crème fraîche and season to taste. Pile the crushed potatoes and artichokes on to warm plates. Rest a pheasant quarter on top of each pile. Spoon the juices with the raisins, mushrooms and lardons around. Tuck a bay leaf between the pheasant and the crushed vegetables to garnish each plate. Serve with carrots and shredded curly kale.

Serves 4

15 g butter
12 shallots, peeled but left whole
50 g lardons (diced bacon)
50 g button mushrooms, thinly sliced
1 cock pheasant, quartered
150 ml chicken stock, ideally fresh or made with ½ stock cube
150 ml fruity white wine
50 g muscatel raisins
1 bay leaf
Salt and freshly ground black pepper
450 g potatoes
350 g Jerusalem artichokes
1 tsp lemon juice
2 tbsp crème fraîche
4 small fresh bay leaves, for garnishing
To serve:
Carrots and shredded curly kale

This is a lovely way of serving your sausages on Christmas Day instead of rolled in streaky bacon in the usual manner. You can cheat and use a ready-prepared vacuum-pack of chestnuts instead of preparing your own, when there is so much to do. But nothing can beat roasting chestnuts on the fire and eating them hot with a little salt!

Brussels sprouts with chestnuts and sausages

Serves 4–6

225 g chestnuts
2 streaky bacon rashers, rinded and
  snipped into small pieces
25 g butter
12 cocktail sausages
350 g–450 g small even-sized
  brussels sprouts (depending on
  how many you'll eat)

1 Prepare the chestnuts in advance. Make a slit in the skin of each one and put the chestnuts in a heavy frying pan on the hob, shaking the pan and turning them occasionally for about 10 minutes until blackened. Alternatively, if you have an open fire, put them on a shovel and cook them traditionally. You could even use the barbecue. When cool enough to handle, peel off the shell and inner skin. Cut into chunky pieces.

2 Wipe the pan (if you used it!) to remove any black dust. Heat it again and fry the bacon bits until crisp and golden. Drain on kitchen paper.

3 Melt just 2 tsp of the butter and fry the sausages for about 5 minutes, turning them, until golden all over and cooked through. Remove from the pan and drain on kitchen paper.

4 Cook the sprouts in boiling, lightly salted water for 4–5 minutes until just tender but still with some 'bite' (larger sprouts will take a few minutes longer). Drain, reserving the stock for any gravy that you're making.

5 Melt the rest of the butter in the sprout pan. Add the sprouts, chestnuts and sausages and toss gently until piping hot and coated in the butter. Tip into a serving dish and sprinkle with the crispy bacon.

These golden, fried, flat cakes are lovely with any grilled meat or fish. Alternatively, serve them topped with a poached or fried egg or some lightly sautéed mushrooms for breakfast, lunch or supper. Wrap the rest of the celeriac in clingfilm and store in the fridge for another day – it will keep well.

Celeriac, potato and parsnip rösti

1   Mix the grated vegetables together in a bowl with the sage and some salt and pepper. Stir in the beaten egg to bind.

2   Heat the oil in a large, non-stick frying pan. Press the mixture into the pan. Fry over a low heat for about 10 minutes until the base of the rösti is golden.

3   Meanwhile, preheat the grill to moderate. Place the pan under the grill and cook for a further 10 minutes until golden and cooked through. Serve straight away cut in wedges.

Serves 4

2 large potatoes, scrubbed and grated
1 parsnip, grated
½ small celeriac, grated
1 onion, grated
2 tsp chopped fresh sage
Salt and freshly ground black pepper
1 egg, beaten
2 tbsp sunflower oil

This is a gorgeous, moist pudding, which is much lighter than most versions. Ideally, make it at the beginning of the month but you can get away with making it right up to the last minute. I have flamed it with Calvados to preserve the apple theme, but brandy or rum will do just as well. If you make one large pudding, steam it for 9 hours.

Flaming Christmas pudding with walnuts, red wine and apples

Makes 2 x 1 litre puddings

700 g mixed dried fruit
100 g shelled walnuts, chopped
1 tbsp red wine
4 Cox's or other eating apples,
    coarsely grated
175 g shredded vegetable suet
100 g soft dark brown sugar
225 g fresh breadcrumbs
2 eggs, beaten
100 g plain flour
1 tsp mixed spice
$\frac{1}{4}$ tsp grated nutmeg
$\frac{1}{4}$ tsp ground cinnamon
$\frac{1}{2}$ tsp grated fresh root ginger
A sprig of fresh holly, a little caster
    sugar and 1 ladleful of Calvados,
    for decorating
To serve:
Cream or custard

1 Put the dried fruit and walnuts in a bowl. Add the wine and leave to soak for 2–3 hours, if possible.

2 Add the apples, suet, sugar and breadcrumbs and mix well. Beat in the eggs. Stir in the flour and spices. At this point, get everyone in the house to stir the pudding and make a wish!

3 Grease two 1 litre pudding basins. Line the bases with a circle of greased greaseproof paper or non-stick baking parchment.

4 Spoon the mixture into the basins and smooth the surface. Cover the surface of each pudding with a circle of greased greaseproof paper or non-stick baking parchment then a saucer or small plate that fits inside the top of the basins. Cover with a double thickness of foil, twisting and folding under the rims to secure. Steam for 7 hours until really dark, topping up with boiling water as necessary.

5 Cool, then cover with clean foil and store in a cool, dark place.

6 When ready to serve, steam for a further 3 hours.

7 To serve, loosen the edge of the pudding with a round-bladed knife, then put a shallow serving dish over the basin. Hold firmly, invert, shake the pudding so you feel it loosen and then remove the basin. Peel off the base paper, if necessary.

8 Put a little foil round the base of the sprig of holly and push into the top of the pudding. Dust the pudding with caster sugar.

9 When everyone is ready, as near to the table as possible, warm the ladleful of Calvados, ignite, pour over the pudding and bring to the table immediately while still flaming. Serve with cream.

Potted Stilton

Stilton cheese is at its best now. Try using some for a fabulous starter or alternative to dessert, served with ripe pears and oatcakes. Mash 100 g of Stilton (without the rind) with 75 g softened unsalted butter, a good pinch of freshly grated nutmeg and $\frac{1}{4}$ tsp English mustard. Work in 2 tbsp rich ruby port. Pack into 6–8 tiny ramekin dishes or 1 larger pot and press down well. Melt a further 75 g unsalted butter and pour over the cheese mixture. Chill until firm.

In my house, this is everyone's favourite Christmas dessert for those who don't enjoy Christmas pudding. It's light but luxurious and completes a festive meal to perfection. You can fill the log with muscatel raisins soaked in rum instead of (or as well as) pears. We always like to add a tiny sprig of holly and a little robin to decorate.

Chocolate and pear yule log

Serves 6–8

175 g plain chocolate (ideally with over 70 per cent cocoa solids)
4 eggs, separated
150 g caster sugar, plus extra for dusting
1 tbsp hot water
3 ripe pears, peeled, cored and finely chopped
150 ml double or whipping cream, whipped
1/4 tsp ground cinnamon
Icing sugar, for dusting

1 Line an 18 x 28 cm Swiss roll tin with non-stick baking parchment so the paper stands at least 2.5 cm above the rim.

2 Melt the chocolate in a bowl over a pan of hot water or melt briefly in the microwave.

3 Whisk the egg whites until stiff. Whisk in 1 tbsp of the caster sugar to stop them 'falling'.

4 Whisk the egg yolks with 75 g of the remaining sugar until thick and pale. Stir in the melted chocolate and the hot water. Fold in the egg whites with a metal spoon.

5 Turn the mixture into the prepared tin and level the surface. Bake in a preheated oven at 180°C/gas 4/fan oven 160°C for about 15 minutes until risen and just firm to the touch.

6 Put a clean tea towel on a board and cover with a sheet of non-stick baking parchment. Dust with a little caster sugar. Turn the cooked chocolate slab out on to the paper and carefully loosen the cooking paper but leave it in place. Cover with a further clean tea towel and leave until cold.

7 Mix the chopped pears with the whipped cream and cinnamon.

8 Remove the cooking paper from the cake and trim the edges with a sharp knife. Spread the pear cream over the cold chocolate slab, not right to the edges. Carefully roll up, using the underneath paper as a guide. Transfer to a serving plate. Dust with a little sifted icing sugar to resemble snow.

Quick reference to foods in season

Foods *in italics* are foods from the UK at the peak of their season.

January
Vegetables: Beetroot, *brussels sprouts, brussels tops, cabbages (green, red, white)*, carrots, celeriac, *celery, chicory*, curly endive, *curly kale, Jerusalem artichokes, leeks*, lettuces, *onions*, pak choi, *parsnips, potatoes (old, maincrop)*, salsify and scorzonera, shallots, spring greens, *swedes*, Swiss chard, turnips.
Fruit and nuts: Apples (Cox's, Bramley), avocados (Fuerte), black grapes, clementines, grapefruit, lemons, mangoes, oranges, passion fruit, *pears (Conference, Comice)*, pineapples, pomegranates, satsumas, Seville oranges, tangerines, walnuts.
Meat, game and poultry: Duck, goose, guinea fowl, *hare, partridge, pheasant (England not Scotland), snipe*, venison, wild duck (mallard), *woodcock*, wood pigeon.
Fish and seafood: Brill, clams, *cockles, cod*, crabs, haddock, hake, halibut, John Dory, lemon sole, monkfish, mussels, oysters, plaice, turbot, *whiting*.

February
Vegetables: *Brussels sprouts, brussels tops, cabbages (green, white*, red), carrots, cauliflowers, celeriac, celery, chicory, *curly endive, curly kale, Jerusalem artichokes, leeks*, lettuces, *onions*, parsnips, potatoes (old or maincrop), *rhubarb (forced)*, salsify and scorzonera, shallots, *spring and winter greens*, swedes, Swiss chard.
Fruit and nuts: Apples (Cox's, Bramleys), avocados (Fuerte), bananas, blood oranges, kiwi fruit, lemons, mangoes, oranges, passion fruit, *pears (Comice)*, pineapples, pomegranates, Seville oranges.
Meat, game and poultry: Guinea fowl, *hare*, suckling pig, venison.
Fish and seafood: *Brill*, brown shrimps, clams, *cockles, cod, cod's roe*, crabs, haddock, hake, halibut, John Dory, lemon sole, *mussels*, oysters, salmon, turbot.

March
Vegetables: *Cabbages (green)*, carrots, cauliflowers, *chicory, leeks*, lettuces, onions, potatoes (old, maincrop), *purple sprouting broccoli, radishes, rhubarb (forced)*, shallots, *spring greens*, spring onions, *swedes*, Swiss chard.
Fruit and nuts: Apples (Cox's, Bramleys), avocados (Fuerte), bananas, blood oranges, kiwi fruit, lemons, mangoes, oranges, passion fruit, pineapples, pomegranates.
Meat, game and poultry: *Hare.*
Fish and seafood: Brown shrimps, *cockles*, cod, hake, John Dory, mussels, oysters, *pollack, salmon*, sea bass, *sea trout*.

April
Vegetables: Broccoli, cabbages (green), *carrots, cauliflowers, garlic*, horseradish, Jersey Royal new potatoes, *lettuces*, morel mushrooms, *purple sprouting broccoli, radishes*, rhubarb, rocket, *sorrel, spinach, spring greens, spring onions, watercress*.
Fruit and nuts: Avocados (Fuerte and Hass), bananas, kiwi fruit, loquats, mangoes, muscat grapes.
Meat, game and poultry: Lamb, *poussins*, rabbit, *wood pigeon*.
Fish and seafood: *Brown shrimps, cockles*, cod, *crabs*, Dublin Bay prawns (scampi), halibut, John Dory, *salmon*, sea bass, *sea trout*.

May

Vegetables: *Asparagus, broad beans*, broccoli, *carrots, cauliflowers, cucumbers, globe artichokes, Jersey Royal new potatoes, lettuces, lovage*, new potatoes, peas, *radishes*, rhubarb, *rocket, sorrel, spinach*, spring onions, *watercress*.
Fruit and nuts: Avocados (Fuerte and Hass), *cherry tomatoes*, cherries, *elderflowers*, kiwi fruit, lychees, mangoes.
Meat, game and poultry: Lamb, *wood pigeon*.
Fish and seafood: Bream, *brown shrimps*, cod, crabs, crayfish, Dover sole, *Dublin Bay prawns (scampi)*, halibut, John Dory, *pollack*, prawns, river trout (brown, rainbow), *salmon*, sea bass, *sea trout*.

June

Vegetables: *Asparagus*, aubergines, *broad beans*, broccoli, *carrots, cauliflowers*, courgettes, cucumbers, Florence fennel, globe artichokes, green garlic, *lettuces*, mangetout, new potatoes, *peas*, pea shoots, *radishes, rhubarb (outdoor)*, rocket, *runner beans, sorrel*, spring onions, turnips, *watercress*.
Fruit and nuts: Avocados (Fuerte and Hass), *cherries, elderflowers, gooseberries*, kiwi fruit, lychees, mangoes, redcurrants, *strawberries*, tomatoes.
Meat, game and poultry: *Lamb*, quail, venison, *wood pigeon*.
Fish and seafood: *Bream*, brown shrimps, cod, *crabs, crayfish*, Dover sole, Dublin Bay prawns (scampi), haddock, halibut, herring, John Dory, lemon sole, lobster, *mackerel*, plaice, *pollack*, prawns, river trout (brown, rainbow), salmon, sardines, *sea bass, sea trout*.

July

Vegetables: *Aubergines, beetroot*, broad beans, broccoli, *carrots, cauliflowers, courgettes, cucumbers, Florence fennel, garlic, globe artichokes, green beans*, green garlic, *herbs, kohlrabi, lettuces, mangetout*, new potatoes, onions, *peas*, peppers, *potatoes (old, maincrop), radishes, rocket*, runner beans, *samphire, sorrel*, sweetcorn, *Swiss chard*, turnips, *watercress*.
Fruit and nuts: Apricots, avocados (Fuerte and Hass), *bilberries/whortleberries*, blackberries, *blackcurrants*, blueberries, *gooseberries*, greengages, kiwi fruit, loganberries, lychees, mangoes, melons, nectarines, peaches, *raspberries, redcurrants, strawberries*, tomatoes, *white currants*.
Meat, game and poultry: *Lamb*, quail, *rabbit, veal (English)*, venison, *wood pigeon*.
Fish and seafood: Bream, *brown shrimps*, cod, *crabs, crayfish*, Dover sole, *Dublin Bay prawns (scampi)*, haddock, herring, John Dory, lemon sole, *lobster, mackerel*, plaice, *pollack*, prawns, river trout (brown, rainbow), salmon, sardines, *scallops*, sea bass, *sea trout*.

August

Vegetables: *Aubergines, beetroot*, broad beans, *broccoli*, cavolo nero, *carrots, chillies, courgettes*, cucumbers, Florence fennel, garlic, globe artichokes, green beans, kohlrabi, *lettuces*, mangetout, onions, peas, peppers, potatoes (old, maincrop), radishes, *rocket*, runner beans, samphire, sorrel, sweetcorn, Swiss chard, watercress.
Fruit and nuts: Apricots, avocados (Hass), *blackberries, blackcurrants*, blueberries, greengages, *loganberries*, mangoes, *melons*, nectarines, pawpaws, peaches, *plums*, raspberries, redcurrants, tayberries, tomatoes, *white currants*.
Meat, game and poultry: *Grouse*, lamb, quail, *rabbit*, venison, *wood pigeon*.
Fish and seafood: *Bream*, brown shrimps, cod, *crabs, crayfish*, Dover sole, Dublin Bay prawns (scampi), grey mullet, haddock, halibut, herring, John Dory, lemon sole, *lobster, mackerel*, monkfish, plaice, *pollack*, red mullet, *river trout (brown, rainbow)*, salmon, sardines, *scallops*, sea bass, *squid, whitebait*.

September
Vegetables: *Aubergines, beetroot, broccoli, butternut squash,* cardoons, *carrots,* celery, *chillies, courgettes, cucumbers, curly kale, Florence fennel, garlic, globe artichokes, kohlrabi,* leeks, lettuces, *mangetout, marrows, onions, peppers, potatoes (old, maincrop),* radishes, *rocket, sweetcorn, Swiss chard, watercress, wild mushrooms (blewits, ceps, chanterelles, field, horse, oyster, parasol, puffballs).*
Fruit and nuts: *Apples (Discovery, Russets, Worcester),* avocados (Hass), *blackberries,* chestnuts, clementines, cranberries, *damsons, elderberries, figs, grapes, greengages, hazelnuts,* mangoes, melons, nectarines, pawpaws, peaches, *pears (William), plums, tomatoes.*
Meat, game and poultry: *Duck, goose, grouse, guinea fowl,* lamb, *quail, rabbit,* venison, *wild duck (mallard), wood pigeon.*
Fish and seafood: *Bream, brown shrimps,* clams, cod, *crabs,* Dublin Bay prawns (scampi), grey mullet, haddock, halibut, John Dory, lemon sole, *lobster, mackerel,* monkfish, plaice, *river trout (brown, rainbow),* scallops, sea bass, skate, *squid, turbot.*

October
Vegetables: Aubergines, *beetroot, broccoli, butternut squash, cardoons, carrots, cavolo nero, celeriac, celery, chillies, curly kale, Florence fennel,* globe artichokes, *kohlrabi,* leeks, lettuces, *marrows,* onions, *peppers, potatoes (old, maincrop),* pumpkins, radishes, *rocket, swedes,* Swiss chard, *turnips,* watercress, *wild mushrooms (blewits, ceps, chanterelles, field, horse, oyster, parasol, puffballs), yams.*
Fruit and nuts: *Apples (Russets, Cox's, Bramleys),* avocados (Hass), *chestnuts, damsons, figs, grapes,* hazelnuts, pawpaws, *pears (Comice, Conference),* quinces, *raspberries (late crop),* tomatoes, walnuts.
Meat, game and poultry: *Duck, goose, grouse, guinea fowl, hare,* lamb, *partridge, pheasant, rabbit, snipe,* venison, *wild duck (mallard),* woodcock, *wood pigeon.*
Fish and seafood: Bream, brill, brown shrimps, clams, *crabs,* Dublin Bay prawns (scampi), *eels,* grey mullet, haddock, hake, halibut, John Dory, lemon sole, *lobster, mackerel,* monkfish, *mussels, oysters,* plaice, *river trout (brown, rainbow),* scallops, *sea bass, squid, turbot.*

November
Vegetables: *Beetroot, butternut squash,* cabbages (green, red, white), *cardoons, carrots, cavolo nero, celeriac, celery, chicory, curly kale, Jerusalem artichokes, kohlrabi, leeks,* lettuces, *parsnips, potatoes (old, maincrop),* pumpkins, *salsify and scorzonera, shallots, swedes,* Swiss chard, *turnips,* watercress, white truffles, *wild mushrooms (blewits, horse, oyster).*
Fruit and nuts: *Apples (Russets, Cox's, Bramleys),* avocados (Fuerte and Hass), *chestnuts,* cranberries, dates, *medlars,* pears (Comice, Conference), persimmons, *quinces, raspberries (late crop), sloes,* walnuts.
Meat, game and poultry: Duck, *goose, grouse, guinea fowl, hare, partridge, pheasant, rabbit, snipe,* venison, woodcock, *wood pigeon.*
Fish and seafood: Bream, brill, clams, *cod, crabs,* Dublin Bay prawns (scampi), *haddock,* hake, halibut, John Dory, lemon sole, *lobster,* monkfish, *mussels, oysters,* plaice, *scallops,* sea bass, *squid,* turbot.

December
Vegetables: Beetroot, *brussels sprouts,* cabbages (green, red, white), cardoons, *carrots,* cauliflowers, *celeriac, celery, chicory, curly kale, Jerusalem artichokes,* lettuces, *parsnips, potatoes (old, maincrop),* pumpkins, *radicchio, shallots, swedes,* Swiss chard, *turnips,* watercress.
Fruit and nuts: Almonds, *apples (Russets, Cox's, Bramleys),* avocados (Fuerte), *chestnuts,* clementines, cranberries, dates, medlars, passion fruit, pears (Comice, Conference), physalis, pineapples, pomegranates, satsumas, tangerines, walnuts.
Meat, game and poultry: Duck, *goose,* grouse, *guinea fowl, hare, partridge, pheasant,* rabbit, *snipe, turkey, venison,* wild duck (mallard), *woodcock, wood pigeon.*
Fish and seafood: Bream, brill, clams, haddock, hake, halibut, John Dory, lemon sole, monkfish, *mussels, oysters,* plaice, scallops, *sea bass,* turbot.